the cinema of

NANNI MORETTI

dreams and diaries

ewa mazierska & laura rascaroli

WALLFLOWER PRESS LONDON & NEW YORK

First published in Great Britain in 2004 by
Wallflower Press
4th Floor, 26 Shacklewell Lane, London E8 2EZ
www.wallflowerpress.co.uk

Book design by Rob Bowden Design

Printed in Great Britain by Antony Rowe, Chippenham, Wiltshire

CONTENT

LIST OF ILLUSTRATIONS

ACKNOWLEDGEMENTS

We wish to express our gratitude to Nanni Moretti and to Sacher Film for replying to our queries, for supplying the originals of the stills and for granting us permission to reproduce them. Our special thanks go to Tom Carroll and Gifford Kerr for their support and for helping us with the editing of the text.

We are also pleased to acknowledge the contribution of the following people, who have helped us in various ways: Adam Wyzynski at the National Film Archive, Poland; Vittorio Bufacchi, Mary Noonan and Aisling O'Leary at the National University of Ireland, Cork; Alba Bariffi at Longanesi, Milan; Matteo Zambetti and the staff of the Associazione Alasca, Torre Boldone (Bergamo).

Archival research in Italy was funded by the Faculty of Arts Research Fund of the National University of Ireland, Cork.

To my children, Kamila and Daniel, and to my nephew Maciej (EM)
To my parents, Ariberta and Adelmo, and to my brother Luca (LR)

I am not a director. I am one who makes films when he has something to say.
                                                        – Nanni Moretti

INTRODUCTION

One of the most outstanding figures in contemporary European and world cinema, Nanni Moretti is the most important Italian film-maker of the past thirty years, not only for his creation of an utterly unique and modern filmic style, or his impact on the national cinematographic industry and his influence on young film-makers, but also for his ability to raise debate, within the world of cinema and also in society at large. These achievements are partly the result of Moretti's unusual position of semi-outsider within the Italian and European cinematographic industry, a position he holds despite the national and international success of many of his films and the influence he now exercises through his own production company, his distribution company, his annual Film Festival and his cinema theatre in Rome. Moretti is still widely seen as an 'autarchic' director – one who has not only 'made it' from his position of outsider, but who also has not bought into the system, and has in fact bent it to his will and used it on his own terms.

Born in Brunico (Bolzano) in 1953, while his parents were on holiday, but resident in Rome, the son of a university professor of Greek Epigraphy (Luigi Moretti, who appeared as an actor in *La sconfitta*, *Io sono un autarchico*, *Ecce Bombo*, *Bianca*, *La messa è finita* and *Palombella rossa*) and of a secondary school teacher (Agata Apicella, who plays herself in *Aprile*), in his youth Nanni Moretti soon developed three of his major interests: politics, the cinema and water polo. While attending the *liceo classico* he played in the water polo league with Lazio and even made the Junior National Team. In those years, he was also active in the extra-parliamentary left – an experience after which he left active politics (by his own admission, he always voted for the Italian Communist Party, without ever being a member), only to return to it in recent times, as we will discuss in the concluding chapter of this book.

Upon finishing secondary school he began to devote himself more seriously to cinema. Being unable to join the Centro Sperimentale per la Cinematografia in Rome, for which he would have needed a university degree, he tried without success to work as an assistant director; then in 1973, at twenty years of age, he sold his stamp collection, bought a Canon Super-8 camera and started to make his own films – a highly unusual debut in the world of film-making. This choice was necessitated by the difficulty of making a more 'regular' debut within the system (cf. De Bernardinis 2001: 35), but is also symptomatic of a structural fault in the Italian cinema industry:

> There's no film industry in Italy. A film-maker devotes five per cent of his effort to the film, and 95 to asking, begging, seeking, phoning, replacing the producer, the distributor, the press-agent, who cannot do their job. Producers in Italy live barricaded in their offices, hoping that nobody is ever going to knock on their doors to propose a film. (Moretti quoted in De Bernardinis 1998: 8)

At the time of Moretti's debut, the only way in which a new director could find funding for an endeavour which was not primarily commercial was often through the famous 'Article 28', introduced in 1965, which offered the state's financial support (to a maximum of 30 per cent of the costs of production) to films 'of cultural interest'. It is thanks to this incentive that film-makers such as Silvano Agosti, Mario Martone, Tullio Giordana and Moretti himself found support for their first films. Nevertheless, the network for the distribution and exhibition of quality films, envisaged by this law, was never implemented. Having managed to self-produce his first films, Moretti found an atypical, 'autarchic' way of reaching an audience – through the so-called 'cineclubs', alternative theatres that enjoyed in Italy an important period of success in the 1970s. Moretti's first three shorts were shot with the help of a group of friends, self-produced and distributed precisely in this way. *La sconfitta* and *Paté de bourgeois* were made in 1973, first shown at the Circolo Nuova Sinistra in Rome, and then at the Venice Film Festival, as part of a programme devoted to underground cinema; *Come parli frate?* (1974) was first projected at the Roman cineclub L'Occhio, l'Orecchio, la

Young Moretti with his Super-8 camera

Bocca, and was the parody of a masterpiece of Italian literature, Alessandro Manzoni's *I promessi sposi*. In the meantime, Moretti was offered a small role in *Padre padrone* (1977) by the Taviani brothers, whom the film-maker will often include among his mentors – but they refused to allow him to become their assistant because, as they later asserted, after seeing his first shorts they realised that he 'was already a film-maker' (Vittorio Taviani quoted in De Bernardinis 2001: 36).

Ready to shoot a full-length feature, Moretti first tried the customary route – he wrote with a friend, Giorgio Viterbo, a screenplay entitled *Militanza, militanza* and sent it to the State-owned distribution company, Italnoleggio, which after one year rejected the proposal. As Moretti commented later, 'I immediately understood that it would be impossible for me to make a film within the industry. The State company as well as the cooperatives and private producers did not choose a project because they liked the story or the screenplay, but for other reasons that escaped me' (quoted in De Bernardinis 2001: 36). Moretti hence persisted with his 'autarchic' project and in 1976 authored his first full-length feature, *Io sono un autarchico*. This film, which even from the title (meaning 'I am an autarchic') looked like a programme for alternative film-making, as well as a proud manifesto of independence, was first shown at the Roman cineclub FilmStudio, where it met with the approval of the audience and became a cult film, thanks to some favourable reviews and to word-of-mouth. Reprinted in 16mm, distributed at a national level by ARCI (the left-wing Associazione Ricreativa Culturale Italiana) through the network of cineclubs and art-house theatres, and finally shown by one of the national television channels, RAI2, *Io sono un autarchico* gave rise to much interest, contributed to the formation of a devoted audience for Moretti, and paved the way to his next effort, *Ecce Bombo* (1978). Produced by two small companies (one of which, Alphabeta, was owned by three Italian actors, a novelty in the panorama of the Italian film industry), *Ecce Bombo* was an unexpected critical and commercial success (costing 180 million liras, it earned 2 billion liras). Moretti quickly ascended to national fame and also began to be known abroad, particularly in France, a country which immediately warmed to his unique style. *Io sono un autarchico* was shown for a whole month at the Studio des Ursulines, a Parisian cinema theatre; *Ecce Bombo* was presented in the main competition at the Cannes Film Festival and was reviewed very positively by the *Cahiers du cinéma* (cf. Fargier 1978). Moretti had made it, and could now more easily find funding for his subsequent films. He was, officially, inside the system.

Nevertheless, rather than taking advantage of the success of *Ecce Bombo* and immediately making another generational comedy, Moretti waited for three years – the most heated years of Italian terrorism – before returning with a completely different film on the world of the cinema, *Sogni d'oro* (1981). Produced by Renzo Rossellini for Gaumont, in collaboration with the national broadcasting service, presented at the 1981 Venice Film Festival, *Sogni d'oro* is, even more so than *Ecce Bombo*, Moretti's first 'industrial' and 'institutional' film, and it was initially endorsed by the critics – so much so that the jury of the Venice Film Festival, led by Italo Calvino, awarded it the Golden Lion Special Jury Prize. Nevertheless, after the Festival the film failed to receive favourable reviews, and was not a success with audiences either. In artistic terms, of course, the film was not 'institutional' at all, and in fact its lack of success might be due to its refusal to obey the unwritten rules of the system – according to which, once a director has 'made it' and has been accepted by the system, he or she must in turn accept the system and satisfy the audience's expectations. In his career, however, Moretti constantly defied rules and often did the opposite of what was expected of him, in a constant effort to displace the audience. At the same time, by offering consistency in the personality traits of the protagonists of his films, and by reiterating elements that have become almost a 'factory trademark', in a Hitchcockian manner, he always played with and contributed to raising the expectation of the public. Thus, Moretti both set the rules and challenged them. *Sogni d'oro* was a difficult film, full of pain, lacking a sympathetic protagonist – it was becoming more and more difficult to pigeonhole its director as a 'new comedian', as well as the director of the young generation. Furthermore, the film appeared to be 'too ambitious' – many critics, unable to distinguish between Michele Apicella and Nanni Moretti, compared it with a sneer to Fellini's *Otto e mezzo* (*8½*, 1963) and attacked the film-maker for his self-assurance, if not for utter incompetence.

Moretti was ready, once again, to change. Wanting to make a film with a well-developed story, he called Sandro Petraglia, screenplay writer and co-author (with Rulli, Agosti and Bellocchio) of another 'autarchic' film, *Nessuno o tutti* (1975), and together they wrote *Bianca*. Produced by the mainstream company of Achille Manzotti, *Bianca* was, once again, a film that defied conventions, and played with the rules of the thriller as well as with the audience's expectations of his own character, so much so that many spectators refused to believe the final revelation that the protagonist played by Moretti was a paranoid murderer (cf. De Bernardinis 2001: 72–3). The film was shown successfully in the circuit of international festivals, and went down very well with the public. Only one year later Moretti had his next film ready, once again produced by Achille Manzotti. *La messa è finita* (1985) confirmed Moretti's international standing, won the Silver Bear at the 1986 Berlin Film Festival, and was particularly successful with the French critics and audience. It was also the last film that Moretti made 'within the industry'.

In 1987 Moretti founded with Angelo Barbagallo a production company, which they named Sacher Film after the famous cake – homage to one of Michele Apicella's better-known manias. Moretti's choice to become a producer was marked by a polemical attitude: 'I decided to become a producer for this reason also: to react against the pleasure that many feel when faced with the crisis of Italian cinema' (quoted in De Bernardinis 2001: 5). Sacher Film went on to produce not only Moretti's subsequent films, but also those of a number of new Italian film-makers, including the very well-received debuts of Carlo Mazzacurati (*Notte italiana*, 1987), Daniele Lucchetti (*Domani accadrà*, 1988) and Mimmo Calopresti (*La seconda volta*, 1996). In 1991, Moretti restructured an old cinema in Rome and opened it with the name Nuovo Sacher, to show, in the film-maker's words, 'either those films that would not find space in Rome, or those that find it difficult to reach their audience' (quoted in De Bernardinis 2001: 122). This quote suggests that it is the brand name 'Sacher' (and hence 'Moretti') that gives authority to texts that would otherwise lose the war against mainstream films and be missed by their potential public. Moretti also founded in 1996 the Sacher Festival, devoted to shorts, which, along with his production company, strengthens his position as a 'father figure' and talent scout for Italian cinema. In 1997 Moretti, together with Angelo Barbagallo, Roberto Cicutto and Luigi Musini, founded the distribution company Tandem, finally reaching complete control of the whole system of production, distribution and exhibition of films. After his debut 'outside the system', and after a series of films made within the industry, the film-maker has now become 'a unique case of an author who can allow himself absolute independence and autonomy in the creation, production and even distribution of his films, achieving the denial of the customary promotional and mediatic rites, leaving entirely to the film the role of "signification"' (Marangi 1999: 21). The popular film magazine *Ciak* has recently ranked Moretti in fifth place on the list of the most powerful names of Italian cinema, in a scale that takes into account the state of the market, stardom and box office success (Porro 2001: 27).

Finally, Moretti's status as auteur, which was never unanimously conceded to him in Italy (denied on the claim that Moretti does not make films but narcissistic texts that are impossible to catalogue or study as a coherent opus), was instead immediately recognised in France by the enthusiastic critics of the *Cahiers du cinéma* and *Positif*. According to *Positif*, for instance, 'Moretti is the greatest Italian director of the last two decades' (Valens 1999: 175). In 1993 the Toronto Film Festival organised the showing of his complete oeuvre. Even the establishment *The Economist* has recently praised Moretti in an article on the rebirth of Italian cinema ('The Moment is Now', 2002: 1). The Palme d'Or for *The Son's Room* received at the 2001 Cannes Film Festival is a further sanctioning of Moretti's credentials at an international level.

Such an intriguing mix of autarchy and authority, self-sufficiency and power, places Moretti's cinema simultaneously at the margins and at the centre of contemporary film production, a paradoxical position which perhaps explains the vision that Moretti has of his own film-making: 'I am not a director. I am one who makes films when he has something to say' (quoted in Comuzio 1986: 63).

From the margins to the centre

Defined by a critic as 'Italy's last diva' because of 'his charismatic, star-like presence' (Young 2002a: 57), Moretti is undeniably a star, and his off-screen appeal has recently shone in his newfound political activism. After unexpectedly taking the podium at the end of a political rally in Piazza Navona in Rome on 2 February 2002 and accusing the leaders of the left of ineffectiveness, thus giving vent to the long-repressed rage of many Italian left-wing voters, Moretti has become one of the most active and representative leaders of the popular movements of protest against the present Berlusconi government. To those who are familiar with and fond of his work, this public exposure and personal commitment is an obvious continuation and radicalisation of the critical and political discourse carried forward through his films. For many others, most of whom dislike Moretti's cinema, his new activism is a sign of his enormous narcissism, if not an improper interference – according to the point of view by which the artist should remain in his or her place and should not engage with discourses outside that which is perceived to be the 'artistic field'.

This divergence of opinion is symbolic of the way in which Moretti and his films have been received in Italy ever since his cinematographic debut. The audience has always been either wholly with him or wholly against him, in a game that apparently excluded the possibility of holding intermediate positions. It must be remarked that such a split has been encouraged by the film-maker himself who, particularly at the beginning of his career, took very clear positions, overtly criticised the shortcomings of the Italian cinematic industry and well-liked mainstream genres such as 'comedy Italian-style', and passionately presented himself as the only noteworthy novelty in the stagnant panorama of Italian film. Not only did Moretti attract much aversion by never concealing, neither in his films nor in interviews, his opinions on the cinema, on contemporary Italian culture and society, as well as on political parties of the right and of the left; since his debut he created and played a critical and intractable character presenting strong autobiographical traits, called in turn Michele Apicella (from his mother's maiden name), Don Giulio, Nanni and Giovanni (the name on his birth certificate), which put himself at the forefront of his cinematic discourse, exposing him to the criticism of many. We have already suggested, for instance, that the direct identification of the director with his protagonist is one of the causes of a commercial fiasco like *Sogni d'oro* – significantly, this is a film in which Moretti appears to be entirely 'himself', because in it he plays a film-maker who is praised for his successful debut film about the young generation. Many people attached Michele Apicella's narcissistic and intractable demeanour in *Sogni d'oro*, not unreasonably, to Moretti's off-screen persona. Moretti was, of course, well-aware of this. It is our belief that Moretti has purposefully exploited the media in order to avoid being exploited by them. As we will suggest and expound in the course of this study, one of the greatest achievements of this director does not lie in his ability to present a truthful self-portrait in his films, but to erase the boundaries between his on-screen and off-screen personas, thus exploring and challenging the meaning itself of autobiography.

With their unusual mix of autobiography and fiction, private observations and social commentary, comedy and tragedy, self-criticism and ferocious satire, Moretti's films are impossible to pigeonhole and to compare to anything else, something which obviously bothers and challenges the less refined critic and the spectator accustomed to mainstream cinema. A reviewer of *Bianca* at the time of the film's release declared that he refused to see Moretti's previous films (implicitly admitting to a preconceived refusal based on Moretti's public persona – or on his portrait by the media), and commented as follows:

> There is no storyline, but it seems that this is typical of Moretti … There is only him, the Moretti-Michele character … [who] is completely devoid of development; he is, as I described him, schematic and didactic, from beginning to end, so much so that after two minutes anybody could replace Moretti and lead the film to its unhappy end. (Fini 1984: 165)

Moretti's films do not fit into any genre: *Bianca*, for instance, is a noir of sorts, but – as the quoted reviewer complains – is devoid of a traditional storyline. Moreover, all his films are fragmentary, full of surreal moments, and completely centred on the main character. Moretti's first two films, *Io sono un autarchico* and *Ecce Bombo*, were generally described by critics as comedies, but already with some difficulty; *Sogni d'oro* was widely perceived – and, as we have seen, with much annoyance – as Moretti's attempt to make his own Fellini's *Otto e mezzo*. With some significant exceptions, critics generally dismissed his films as being 'ugly', unrefined, badly shot and edited, and accused them of being 'home cinema' rather than professional products.

Just as they do not correspond to the parameters of genre and of mainstream production, Moretti's films do not fit easily in the category of art-house cinema, which since the 1970s has developed into a 'genre' of its own, with rather polished and standardised products aimed at a specific (middle class and educated) audience. Moretti's cinema is not straightforwardly indebted to the tradition of art-house European cinema from a narrative and stylistic perspective; furthermore it shuns the production and distribution methods adopted by contemporary art-house films.

Discussing in similar terms the question of the categorisation of Moretti's work, Rino Genovese suggested that it could be read as 'idiosyncratic cinema'

– in the sense of cinema of the diversity of the individual from the rest of the world (cf. Genovese 1999). The definition suggests the isolation of Moretti in the panorama of world cinema, as well as a limitation of horizons which is simultaneously a weakness and a point of strength. As the same critic suggests, 'The only price that Moretti in his autarchic rigor is forced to pay is the limitedness of its ray of influence … Moretti's films rather talk about Italy and about living in Italy as a torment and an ordeal for an Italian' (Genovese 1999: 71). It is certainly true that Moretti's films speak about the Italian character and about contemporary Italy, and that their success abroad is partly due to this characteristic – foreign audiences probably enjoy his films and laugh at Moretti's gestures and body language, as well as at the situations he portrays, partly because they appear to be so 'Italian'. On the other hand, Moretti's cinema does succeed in speaking to non-Italian spectators on a more general plane, by virtue of its modernity or, better still, of its postmodernity. Moretti's cinema is one of the most effective representations of life in Western Europe today, because of its ability to reprocess both high and popular culture (from Fellini and Pasolini to pop songs and *Doctor Zhivago*); to be utterly eclectic and hybrid in its combination of heterogeneous discourses; to encourage the spectator's reflection by breaking the fiction through the use of surrealism, of documentary, and of direct interpellation of the audience; to formulate a very refined discourse on the subtle distinctions between documentary and fiction, between private sphere and public sphere, and between self-portrait and portrait of the world; and, ultimately, to demystify authority and to reject grand ideological or religious explanations of life, and look at it instead from a personal and contingent viewpoint. We argue that Moretti's very 'marginality' (of geographical position, of discourse, of style and of methods) pushes him to the centre of contemporary film production, just as happens to other radical postmodern authors of world cinema, including Abbas Kiarostami, Aki Kaurismäki, Atom Egoyan and Lars von Trier. In this post-ideological society it is those authors who reflect on the world and on the cinema with full awareness of their contingent viewpoint that truly speak to the contemporary spectator and stretch his or her viewing and moral position – as Ien Ang suggests, it is by marginalising oneself that one can start relating to others in new, more modest and dialogic ways (cf. Ang 1992).

Although Moretti's cinema seems to be 'unique' and difficult to relate to anything else, his films do not subsist in a vacuum and are indebted to the work of many other directors. Moretti's style is mainly connected to radicalism; whereas its autobiographical quality is unique in both mainstream and art-house film-making and draws on experimental authors such as Stan Brakhage, its metacinematic aspect reminds us of the early films by Jean-Luc Godard, where characters also made comments on cinema and political issues while looking straight into the lens. In interviews, Moretti has often drawn attention to his love for the unrealistic, experimental films of Carmelo Bene, as well as of the most radical political cinema of the 1960s – that made by the Taviani brothers, Bellocchio, Pasolini, Ferreri, Bertolucci and the French *nouvelle vague* (cf. Giovannini, Magrelli & Sesti 1986: 8, 33–4, 38). In other words, a cinema that was strongly anti-establishment in character. In common with them, Moretti makes films that are experimental, non-aligned, provocative and anti-dogmatic – in other terms, that are located in the sphere of counter cinema. We will discuss this topic more in depth in the concluding chapter of this book.

On the other hand, Moretti is also indebted to Italian post-war Neorealism, and in particular to its theorist, Cesare Zavattini. As we will suggest and elucidate in the first chapter, Zavattini's most radical neorealist and post-neorealist suggestions are evoked by Moretti's diary-films, *Dear Diary* and *Aprile*, as well as by the diary-shorts *L'unico paese al mondo* (1994) and *Il giorno della prima di 'Close Up'* (Opening Day of *Close-Up*, 1996).

Moretti's cinema as a crossroads of discourses

In this book we will look at Moretti's film-making as the origin and crossroads of a series of heterogeneous discourses of relevance to the sphere of art and to the social order – discourses on style, on contemporary culture and society, on authority, on politics, on language and on the postmodern condition. For this reason, rather than addressing each film and analysing it in depth, we favour a more flexible approach that, we believe, will produce a more coherent vision of Moretti's work, but that will also allow us to address such discourses almost independently of Moretti's cinema, although through the lens that his cinema offers. Our analysis will focus on four fundamental themes that traverse and inform his oeuvre: autobiography, the diary, and the representation of the artist in film; the crisis of the family and of masculinity in Italy and in the Western world; comedy, humour, radical satire and existential irony; the transformation of the citizen's relationship to the polity in Western societies and the importance of language in postmodern politics.

While addressing these four key topics, we will situate Moretti's films within the framework of the Italian and European cinematic industry and of the history of Italian cinema from the 1970s to date. Thus, at the same time as offering an in-depth study of Moretti's films, we will look at his oeuvre as an example of the articulation of the relationship between cinematic radicalism and the establishment of the production and distribution of films in contemporary Europe. We will also firmly situate Moretti's films within their socio-political and historical context, thus studying them as a commentary on the transformations of Italian and Western European society over the past thirty years. We will explore important formal features of Moretti's cinema – the ways in which he both constructs and effaces an effect of reality and mixes autobiography and fiction will be discussed in depth in the first and in the fourth chapters, but will also be developed elsewhere, and in particular in the second chapter; his use of humour and comedy and his construction of absurd or grotesque situations and images will form the subject matter of the third chapter; his camera style, his use of space and time, and his cinema's relationship with that of other film-makers will be analysed particularly in the final chapter, in the section entitled 'Moretti's cinema as counter cinema' (see also note 4 to the first chapter); the incorporation of other media and of their discourses and the question of the relationship of Moretti's cinema to radical postmodern modes of narration and representation will emerge over and over again. As well as the four fundamental themes – autobiography, family, irony and politics – other topics will be extensively discussed, such as Moretti's commentary on the modern mass media and on popular culture; his criticism of mainstream Italian genres such as the *commedia all'italiana* (comedy Italian-style); and the relationship of his work with the tradition of political cinema. We will also examine Moretti's stance on universal problems such as the meaning and value of human life, and his philosophical position as a liberal ironist. Finally, we aspire to contribute to the understanding of the postmodern condition in Western society, through an analysis of aspects of it such as the crisis of masculinity and of authority, the crisis of the left and the transformation of the political discourse.

The image of Moretti's cinema that will emerge from our work will be one of coherence of themes and of attitude, but also of transformation and growth. As we will show in the course of our work, Moretti was 'already a film-maker' at his debut – so much so that a critic, commenting on *Io sono un autarchico*, wrote: 'It may have taken Chaplin several years to develop the Tramp, but here Michele, Moretti's alter ego in seven subsequent films, is already fully realised' (Young 2002a: 57). Although maintaining a highly consistent vision over the course of his career, Moretti as a film-maker also progressed and 'matured', both in terms of style and of his vision of life – to the extent that his films can be read as the diary of the life and growth of one person. In this light, even his latest, *The Son's Room*, heralded by most critics as a film which is utterly different from Moretti's previous work, is instead the logical continuation of many of Moretti's habitual discourses. As Moretti once declared: 'My ambition? I hope I will always make the same film, if possible more and more beautiful' (quoted in Giovannini, Magrelli & Sesti 1986: 39).

A note to the reader

At the end of this book an appendix may be found with the technical details of the films that Moretti directed, as well as a collection of brief synopses. We hope that this will be useful, particularly for those readers who are not familiar with each and every one of Moretti's films, few of which have been distributed to date in the English-speaking world. In the course of our work we will avoid extended descriptions of the films' plots, in the knowledge that readers may refer to the appendix for further details.

Because we chose to devote the chapters of our monograph to specific themes, each of Moretti's films is discussed several times, in different chapters and from different perspectives. We adopted this approach in the conviction that it would produce a more focussed discussion of Moretti's cinema as an organic and meaningful oeuvre. Precise referencing to individual films can be found in the book's index.

Moretti's films will be quoted throughout with their original title, unless they were distributed in the UK with an English title – this being the case of only two features, *Dear Diary* (*Caro diario*) and *The Son's Room* (*La stanza del figlio*), and of the short *Opening Day of 'Close-Up'* (*Il giorno della prima di 'Close Up'*).

All translations from texts in languages other than English are by the authors.

CHAPTER ONE

Nanni Moretti's Self-Portrait as a Humble Artist

With myself I have nothing in common.
— Franz Kafka

It is not because of conceit that I said that I would like to make films about myself. It was simply the only thing I was able to do.
— Nanni Moretti

Does autobiography exist?

All critics who discuss Nanni Moretti's cinema draw attention to the fact that it is largely autobiographical and meta-cinematic. In this chapter we will examine these claims; before we begin our investigation, it is necessary to establish what it means for a film (or any work of art) to be autobiographical.

Attempts were made to distinguish 'autobiography' from related literary forms, such as the personal essay, the diary, the travel journal, the autobiographical novel and the memoir, but for the purpose of this chapter we will pay no attention to the differences existing between them, and will regard them as different examples of the same genre of 'autobiography'.[1] The dictionary definition of autobiography is a work of art whose subject is the author's own life. This definition is as simple as it is burdened with problems. Some critics argue that all art is autobiographical, because even if it does not represent facts from the life of an artist as perceived by outsiders (including art historians), it nevertheless reveals his or her 'inner life', ideas and emotions. Yet, if we accept this claim, the very concept of autobiography ceases to be methodologically viable. Therefore, it is necessary either to put further restrictions on the concept of autobiography (such as the demand that the artist confirm that a given film, painting or novel represents his life); or to discriminate autobiography in a wider sense (by which all art is autobiographical) and in a narrower sense (by which only some novels, paintings and films are autobiographical), and concentrate solely on the latter.

A second, contrasting argument claims that no work of art can be auto-biographical, because it is impossible to represent oneself completely and accurately; representations are the product of selection and abstraction, therefore they are always and inevitably subjective and partial. In order to show the director's life, for example, a film would have to last as long as the life itself and fulfil many conditions that present problems which are logically or technically insurmountable. Moreover, the artist of whom the film is a biography or autobiography, even if played by him or herself, in the process of film-making changes into a symbol which replaces the actual person. The viewer might not even be aware that the film was intended as an autobiography of the author, or may regard the references to his life as meaningless. In this case, the spectator could interpret the film as being about something different – such as love, jealousy, childhood or some other universal human condition. Some autobiographical films (in common with literary autobiographies) do not even mention the fact that the film's protagonist is a film-maker, or they do it in such a way that the uninformed viewer might fail to notice the autobiographical element. Such films, including *Zerkalo* (*Mirror*, 1974) by Andrei Tarkovsky and *Fanny och Alexander* (*Fanny and Alexander*, 1982) by Ingmar Bergman, as Wendy Everett observes, are typically regarded by the viewers as films about their own childhood rather than that of the film's author (Everett 1996).

What is more, there are additional philosophical problems with the concepts of human 'life' and 'identity'. As Szymon Wrobel observes,

> 'Life', in common with a narrative, is the construct of human imagination in the same way as any other narrative. When somebody tries to relate his/her life to us, it is always a certain cognitive achievement, not a statement of things which simply happened. It is also a narrative achievement. From a psychological point of view, life as such does not exist; those who relate it select the events and interpret them at the same time. From the philosophical perspective, one cannot be a naive realist regarding one's own life. (Wrobel 2001: 149)

Wrobel, recalling contemporary ideas and notions promulgated by such authors as Slavoj Zizek and Homi Bhabba, suggests that human 'life' and 'identity' be regarded as products of the narration of one's life, and that stories about one's life not be regarded as being a consequence of living a particular life and of having a particular identity. If we accept Wrobel's argument, then to establish that a work of art is an autobiography ultimately requires a matching of one partial and subjective representation with another representation, which is also partial and subjective. A similar argument is presented by Stuart Hall who, drawing on the works of some twentieth-century thinkers, including post-Marxist Louis Althusser and post-Freudian Jacques Lacan, maintains:

> Rather than speaking of identity as a finished thing, we should speak of *identification*, and see it as an on-going process. Identity arises, not so much from the fullness of identity which is already inside us as individuals, but from a *lack* of wholeness which is 'filled' from *outside us*, by the ways we imagine ourselves to be seen by *others*. Psychoanalytically, the reason why we continually search for 'identity', constructing biographies which knit together the different parts of our divided selves into a unity, is to recapture this fantasised pleasure of fullness (plenitude). (Hall 1992: 287–8)

Adam Phillips, who also draws on psychoanalysis, says: 'The autobiographer is doubly disabled. Without psychoanalytical interpretation there is no personal history, only its concealment. According to this view, those who want to continue misleading themselves about the past write autobiographies; those who want to know themselves and their history have psychoanalysis' (Phillips 1994: 60).

To summarise all these views, it appears not only that a true or complete autobiography is impossible, but that there is no absolute template against which any 'flawed' and partial autobiography can be compared. Consequently, instead of trying to establish whether any film by Moretti is autobiographical or not, we will talk about 'autobiographical effect', meaning with this expression the viewer's impression to be watching the life of the film's author. We will attempt to discern the means through which the impression of the verisimilitude of the cinematic representation and of the artist's own life and character is achieved. Our argument is that autobiography is not only a question of content, but also of form and style. For this reason, special attention will be given to the diary as one of the principal forms that Moretti adopts to communicate with the audience.

As much as the artist's autobiography is shaped by his actual life, so his actual life (or what is regarded to be his life) is shaped by his autobiography. The critics who discuss autobiography in Moretti's work, the majority of whom never met the artist in person, operate a concept of 'Moretti' that seems to be largely influenced by his films (somewhat as those art historians who base their opinions about Rembrandt's or Van Gogh's personalities and lives on the artists' self-portraits and on their general oeuvres). For example, the real Moretti is typically described as a left-wing, neurotic and eccentric person obsessed by shoes and addicted to chocolate cake, largely because these features are present in a number of the characters he has played. Thanks to an elaborate game of recurrence and variation of details, Moretti's films seen together convey two contrasting impressions – that their protagonists are different incarnations of a single individual, and that they are various stages in the development of the same person. This double effect reinforces the conviction that all Moretti's films talk about a particular individual, identified with the film-maker himself, who is either playing at exhausting all the possible lives he could have lived (as a political activist, a teacher, a priest, an MP, a psychoanalyst or a film director), or who is writing an artistic (in the sense of partly fictional) diary of his own development, from youth to maturity. This is why the genius of this film-maker lies not so much in accurately representing himself, but in convincing us that the main protagonist of his films is their author.

In interviews the director himself supports the idea that his films contain many autobiographical elements. On the other hand, he warns against confusing his cinema with his life and emphasises that even his most autobiographical pictures are not documentaries about himself, because they add and extract elements to and from his biography – and also because films are, by their very nature, artificial (cf. Porton & Ellickson 1995). Moreover, in many of Moretti's films the autobiographical elements are not concentrated in one character, but are somehow distributed between the main protagonist and his antagonists. As Moretti says in an interview, 'I consider my characters and the other characters to be complementary, like two sides of a coin. Instead, the words that I said as an actor came to be seen as my view as a director. There's frequently this misunderstanding, but it is more common when the director is also the protagonist of the film' (Porton & Ellickson 1995: 14).

One of the reasons why artists produce autobiographies is the natural human desire to 'reproduce' oneself or even to create a better version of oneself. Creating autobiography, in this perspective, is similar to 'producing' a child. With this function are connected two others: catharsis and therapy. By re-inventing oneself in art, the author comes to terms with his past, in analogy with the patient of the psychoanalyst, who overcomes his traumas by recounting his past experiences (cf. Wrobel 2001: 140–5). Autobiographies also feed the hope of finding or of creating unity in a life which is fragmented, displaced and dispersed. Perhaps it is no accident that they proliferate in contemporary, postmodern times, in which dislocation and fragmentation are regarded as the main 'malaises' affecting individuals as well as whole communities (think, for instance, about the spectacular, worldwide success of recent literary diaries, including the semi-autobiographical best-seller of Helen Fielding, *Bridget Jones's Diary*). It could be that the more decentred and fragmented is identity in the life experience of human beings, the more humans find it necessary to make up for this loss through artistic production.

Self-portraits are also regarded as means of publicising one's own work, by furnishing it with a personal 'stamp' or 'logo'. Therefore, they are treated as evidence of the artist's vanity and narcissism. However, the opposite argument can also be presented: creating an autobiography (unlike writing about the 'wider world') suggests modesty on the part of the artist, her desire to talk only about objects which she knows best, and her unwillingness to move towards unknown territory, nor to speculate, generalise or create interpretative theories. The model and artistic pinnacle of such an autobiography even now is *Rememberance of Things Past* by Marcel Proust. By limiting his literary task to describing only himself and his social milieu, Proust conveys in his novel an impression of complete accuracy and genuineness, rarely found in other books. Moreover, paradoxically, as philosopher Richard Rorty observes, by rejecting any authority, or the idea that there is a privileged perspective from which to describe himself or the world, Proust became in his turn an authority for his readers (Rorty 1989: 102–3). We shall return to these opinions on the character of autobiography in due course, when discussing the 'authority' of Moretti's cinema.

Artists and film-makers on screen

Another widely held opinion on Moretti's cinema (an opinion which is usually found intertwined with the claim that it is autobiographical) is that he makes films about films and film-makers. In order to establish Moretti's distinctive attitude to being a film-maker it helps to put his films in the wider context of the representation of artists and directors in films. In her article on 'Artists mythologies and media genius, madness and art history' (1980), Griselda Pollock sets out to establish the main features of the representation of artists in art history, by concentrating on one special case – that of Vincent Van Gogh. Pollock suggests that, being a paradigm of the 'modern artist', Van Gogh can serve as a model of the way in which artists are depicted in art history books and, by extension, in the popular media. She sums up this approach in the term 'psycho-biography': 'Around his [Van Gogh's] life and work what appears to be a particular form of discourse has developed – a special way of discussing the artist and his works which is presented as if it were only a response to a reflection of his exceptional individuality, his genius' (1980: 62). Hence, the artist is characterised by excess, mania, pathology, otherness and, consequently, solitude and tragedy, and his art is regarded as a reflection of these aspects of his personality. Pollock, who is close to the Marxist perspective on art, which emphasises the relationship between artistic production and social, economic and political history, is highly critical of perceiving madness as the main factor of Van Gogh's work, or indeed, of that of any other painter. She suggests that 'the discourse on madness and art operates to sever art and artist from history and to render both unavailable to those without the specialised knowledge of its processes which art history claims for itself' (1980: 65). The popular media and cinema in particular tend to follow art history books when depicting the artist's life (at the expense of his work), and regard the artist's excessive personality as the crucial factor in his art, neglecting other influential aspects, such as socio-political circumstances.

John A. Walker, in his book *Art and Artists on Screen* (1993), agrees that psycho-biography is regarded by art historians as well as by film directors as the key to the understanding of an artist's work. Walker, who based his research on a larger group of films about real and fictitious artists, also observes that they tend to emphasise the rift between artists and society:

> The rift gives rise to a whole series of conceptions of artists as beings who are *different* from ordinary people: they are inspired geniuses, eccentrics, bohemians, lunatics, outsiders, rebels, iconoclasts and scourges of the bourgeoisie (upon whom, paradoxically, they usually rely for financial support) … Artists preserve in their practice something society in general has lost, for example control over their work, pride and pleasure in their labour. They are still in touch with unconscious desires and forces – the erotic, the perverse, the obscene and the blasphemous – which 'straight' society has outlawed or repressed. They also invoke archaic and primitive forms – pagan religions, magic, alchemy, the occult, shamanism – which rational, scientific society considers it as transcended. The artist thus becomes a repository of values which mainstream society has relinquished. (Walker 1993: 16)

No wonder there is conflict between artists and society; typically, society is unable to appreciate or even to understand the new, unusual way of perceiving the world which an artist proposes. On the other hand, the artist rejects compromise, even at the price of failing to gain widespread recognition and financial success. In the films that Walker analyses, justice is always on the artist's side, of which the ultimate proof are his or her posthumous fame and large following of imitators.

There is no separate study concerning the way in which film directors and mass-media artists and professionals are portrayed in the cinema, although one can enumerate dozens of films made on this subject, particularly since the beginning of the New Waves in the late 1950s and early 1960s. In this period the cinema started to question its own nature, status, relationship with reality and with other media (particularly television) and, consequently, to examine its own creators. Examples are *Otto e mezzo* (*8½*, 1963) by Federico Fellini, *Le Mepris* (*Contempt*, 1963) by Jean-Luc Godard, *Blow-Up* (1966) by Michelangelo Antonioni, *Wszystko na sprzedaz* (*Everything for Sale*, 1968) by Andrzej Wajda, and *La nuit Americaine* (*Day for Night*, 1973) by François Truffaut. Interest in film-making and film-makers grew even more in the following decades, when postmodernism dominated art cinema – examples are numerous films by such versatile authors as Americans Woody Allen, the Coen Brothers and Alexander Rockwell; Iranian Abbas Kiarostami; Canadian-Armenian Atom Egoyan; British Derek Jarman; Polish Marek Koterski; as well as later works of directors with strong meta-cinematic interests such as Federico Fellini (*Intervista*, 1987) and Jean-Luc Godard (*For Ever Mozart*, 1996; *Eloge de l'amour*, 2001).

In the vast majority of films about film-makers, the latter are usually portrayed in a manner different from the way in which painters are treated in the cinema. With few exceptions (including the autobiographical films of Derek Jarman, and particularly *The Garden*, which foreground the film-maker's mental and physical pain, caused by AIDS)[2] there is a lesser tendency to present film-makers as lonely and suffering geniuses, misunderstood and maltreated by society. This attitude is partly explained by the fact that few film directors reached such a mythical status as did Rembrandt or Van Gogh. Moreover, those who achieved success did not need to wait until decades after their death. The greatest, such as Sergei Eisenstein and Orson Welles, typically gained recognition during their lifetime, after their first or second film. A large portion of films about film-makers concerns artists of average ability or the positively talentless, who are portrayed as vain, craving publicity and jealous of the success of their colleagues. Take, for example, Woody Allen's *Crimes and Misdemeanors* (1989), which concerns two film-makers, played respectively by Alan Alda and by Woody Allen himself, one of whom is a showy producer of cheap entertainment without any artistic value whatsoever, the other an author of pretentious and boring documentaries with no hope of attracting a wider audience. Other examples include Tim Burton's *Ed Wood* (1994), about the director of *Glen or Glenda* and *Plan Nine from Outer Space*, who is often described as the world's worst film-maker; *Boogie Nights* (1997) by Paul Thomas Anderson, about Jack Horner, successful director of porno movies; and *Gods and Monsters* (1998) by Bill Condon, which is a fictionalised biography of James Whale, the ex-pat British director of Hollywood horror movies such as *Frankenstein* and *Bride of Frankenstein*. Whale's films are hardly masterpieces or paragons of cinematic authorship. Watching Condon's film one even feels that the director of *Bride of Frankenstein* enjoyed greater luxury and status than he deserved.

The many faces of Michele Apicella

The terms 'biography' and 'autobiography' were first used in relation to Moretti's cinema following the premiere of *Ecce Bombo*, his first full-length feature film (Auty 1979: 170), and subsequently used with reference to the majority of his later films, as well as to his Super-8 debut, *Io sono un autarchico*. At the same time, there is consensus amongst the critics that, from the perspective of autobiography, Moretti's oeuvre should be divided into two parts: films in which he plays himself, and films in which he is replaced by another character. The second part also consists of two subgroups: films with Michele Apicella, who can be regarded as Moretti's alter ego, and films in which the relationship between the protagonist and the director hardly exists at all. The last group is to date represented only by Moretti's latest film, *The Son's Room*, which has little relevance to the question of autobiography, and therefore will not be touched upon by our analysis. In this section we will turn our attention to the 'Apicella films'.

At first sight, this group is very heterogeneous: Moretti impersonates men of different ages and occupations, such as a student, a film-maker, a teacher, a priest, a politician and a sportsman. Such a variety of characters seems to suggest that these are portraits of different people, rather than of the same person. Yet, in a psychoanalytical model, to which Moretti alludes in many of his films, 'in so far as people have a dominant story about who they are, they have a repetitive story. And repetition, for Freud, is forgetting in its most spellbinding form' (Phillips 1994: 69). Hence, paradoxically, the fact that Moretti offers us characters who are apparently different, but are linked by a dominant story, is an argument in favour of the opinion that in his films he constructs his true autobiography. For example, all the protagonists have similar family situations: in spite of being adult they still live either with their mother/parents or by themselves. Their emotional lives are always in turmoil: they simultaneously love and hate their birth family. Each of them also loves a woman (typically her name is Silvia, which is also the name of Moretti's partner in real life), but at the same time is unwilling or unable to approach her, or rejects her when she offers him her affection, something that happens both in *Sogni d'oro* and in *Bianca*. Furthermore, many of these men can be described as idealists: they think about improving society, they possess or seek to possess utopian visions, they are politically active, and they proselytise. In addition, the majority of Apicellas think in a 'cinematic way' – their language is saturated with metaphors and expressions derived from films, they care a lot about the state of Italian cinema, sometimes they even behave as if they were actors in films, like Michele in *Ecce Bombo* who, when talking to his girlfriend, often uses a 'movie dialogue'. We can also identify consistencies in the *mise-en-scène*: in both *Bianca* and *La messa è finita*, for instance, Michele Apicella lives in a penthouse apartment with a large balcony full of plants – similarly to Nanni and Silvia in *Aprile*.

The 'Apicella films' can also be described as films about constructing an autobiography and acquiring an identity. By various means Michele tries to give unity and meaning to his existence. Sometimes he does so by identifying with the lives of other people, as is the case of *Sogni d'oro*, *Bianca* and, to a certain extent, *La messa è finita*. Another method of constructing an autobiography is the recollection of events from one's past, especially childhood, as in the many flashbacks of *Palombella rossa*; Michele's obsession with his childhood is also evident in other films in which he is practically fixated on his past, as happens in *Sogni d'oro* and, to a lesser extent, in *La messa è finita*. The most likely explanation of Michele's refusal to grow up is his split personality, or even schizophrenia. This condition mirrors Moretti's own schizophrenic position as an author/protagonist of his films, therefore as somebody who must dissect his own life in his films, and who maybe loses his own, true identity in the process. In order to understand the similarities and differences between the various Apicellas in different films, as well as the possible relationships between them and Moretti's off-screen persona, we will discuss in detail three features: *Ecce Bombo*, *Sogni d'oro* and *Palombella rossa*.

The main reason why the protagonist of *Ecce Bombo* is identified with Moretti, aside from being played by the director, is the fact that he represents the socio-cultural milieu of left-wing student activists, with whom Moretti was identified at or about the time of the film's release. Moreover, the anti-realist style of the film, marked by such features as the use of non-professional actors, the lack of a conventional plot and the

Ecce Bombo (1978)

improvised dialogue (or one which feels improvised), bears comparison with non-professional, 'private' cinema. At the same time, *Ecce Bombo* cannot be regarded as a narrative of Moretti's life. The director's himself in interviews has suggested that Michele Apicella is not himself but his alter ego, and that, in spite of the documentary-like feel of *Ecce Bombo*, the events featured in the film are played for the camera and are largely fictional.

While some of the differences between Moretti and his filmic self-image result purely from the limitations of the medium, others reveal his desire to distance himself from the peculiarities of his own personality and situation, in order to focus on larger objects, such as his generation, Italian men of his age, or left-wing radicals. Another, although connected, reason for Moretti to deviate from autobiography is to live an alternative, different life on-screen, and acting out some of his hidden dreams and anxieties. Hence, it is worth drawing attention to the several differences existing between

Apicella and the off-screen Moretti. Firstly, Michele in this film is not a film-maker. We have a suspicion that he dreams of becoming one, as he is very interested in films, but he lacks self-confidence, determination and perhaps the talent to pursue this goal. There is a person in his social circle who embarks on a career in the movies: his girlfriend. The fact that she is a woman who puts her professional success first (she leaves Michele despite his remonstrations in order to shoot a film outside Rome) largely reflects, as Martyn Auty puts it, the problem of 'forging a new role for men in a post-'68/pre-feminist society' (Auty 1979: 170). Secondly, Michele, in common with his group of comrades as a whole, feels politically impotent and lacking in direction. Their all-male meetings do not lead to any ideas for action or even for serious discussion. For example, although Michele and his friends object to the predictable and stereotypical portrait of young people that is conveyed by the local television, they do nothing to contradict it, but rather reinforce it by refusing to be serious when they are interviewed. On the other hand, they are largely unimpressed by the rigid and regimented lifestyle of a leftist commune which they visit. Neither are they able to help their female friend who suffers a mental breakdown. The most powerful symbol of their frustration, impotence and detachment from reality is their adoption of the expression 'Ecce Bombo', which is a foolish degeneration of 'Ecce Homo', as the group's motto. The slogan 'Ecce Bombo' is not even the group's own invention, but is borrowed from an old, eccentric man who rides a bicycle piled high with junk. As Auty observes, the impression of impotence and emptiness is also conveyed intertextually by reference to Buster Keaton: 'His hang-dog expression presides from a poster on Michele's wall – a contemplation of emptiness bequeathed by one frenetic film-maker to another' (Auty 1979: 170).

The crucial problem for Michele Apicella in *Ecce Bombo* is one of identity, of establishing who he is and what his relationships with the world are. Michele (not unlike the protagonist of the first film by Moretti, *Io sono un autarchico*) largely identifies himself with his male friends and lives through them. Hence, the answer to the question 'who am I?' largely depends on the answer 'who are *we*?' and 'who do *we* want to be?' Yet, as time passes, we also observe him loosening ties with his male circle and going through a process of individualisation. The conclusion and epitome of this process is the last episode in the film, in which Michele visits Olga, the schizophrenic friend. He does so on his own, although initially the whole group was meant to visit her.

As a member of a post-1968 generation Moretti might identify with many of the problems addressed in *Ecce Bombo*, but they affect him in a less profound way than other people of his age, gender and background. Paradoxically, the very fact of completing *Ecce Bombo* which, in its category of small-budget, independent production, was a very successful film, is a testimony of the disparity between the real Moretti and his alter ego. The protagonist of *Ecce Bombo* is one in a long line of characters in Moretti's films who are less successful than the director himself. The choice of an impotent radical as the film's protagonist can be interpreted both as a testimony to a self-ironical attitude on the part of Moretti,[3] and as an act of solidarity with those who are less successful and articulate than himself. In one of his later films, *Dear Diary*, Moretti will state: 'I will always feel at ease with a minority.' One possible interpretation of this sentence is that Moretti will always feel in tune with 'losers', like the amiable lot in *Ecce Bombo*.

Despite his claim to be 'a great artist', Michele in *Ecce Bombo* is not a suffering genius. Rather, he should be classified as a young man looking for direction in his life. The protagonist of *Sogni d'oro*, although still young, has already made some important choices in his life and had some significant achievements. He is regarded as the best Italian film director of his generation, who voices the aspirations and anxieties of young people (like the real Moretti at the time of making *Sogni d'oro*). He himself rejects this label, not wanting to be pigeonholed – again in common with the off-screen Moretti. Yet, he simultaneously reveals many symptoms of psychiatric disorder: he is suspicious, neurotic, moody, aggressive and difficult to work with. Despite being at least in his late twenties, Michele Apicella still lives with his mother, who organises and largely dominates his life. His erotic life is limited to dreaming about being emotionally and sexually involved with a woman whom he fears to approach. Moreover, he leads his life more 'in his head' than in reality, dreaming and daydreaming. On many occasions he suggests that his personality is split, that there is another person sharing his mind.

These characteristics might suggest that the protagonist of *Sogni d'oro* approaches the 'suffering genius' model of the representation of artists. However, Moretti's portrait of Apicella, unlike the cinematic representations of Van Gogh or Rembrandt, is largely a caricature of a 'mad genius'. His gestures are exaggerated, he is unpredictable in his behaviour, he is arrogant (he believes that he is the only innovative force in Italian cinema) and at the same time full of self-pity. On many occasions Moretti even suggests that Apicella's talent is questionable. The footage of the film which he is shooting makes rather unappealing viewing: the script lacks drama, the acting is mediocre, to list but a few shortcomings. Furthermore, unlike the archetypal genius, who remains aloof from the outside world, Michele craves appreciation and popularity, which ultimately is a sign of his conformity and insecurity. This is evident in his attitude to a fellow successful director, Gigio Cimino, who embarks on a musical about the Vietnam War. Michele is very contemptuous of this colleague and at the same time is envious of his popularity and, perhaps, of his ability to merge serious content with light form. Nowhere is his attitude better revealed than in the scene in which Michele takes part in a television competition with Gigio Cimino, during which he is defeated and humiliated. On the whole, one must doubt that this caricatured and undignified figure is Moretti as the real director wants us to see him. In the light of the later *Aprile*, in which the director protagonist is unable to choose between two projects, one of which is a musical about a Trotskyite pastry cook, we risk the suggestion that in *Sogni d'oro* Moretti includes his two alter egos: one (Michele) inclined towards art cinema, the other (Gigio) inclined towards a popular and generic cinema, albeit not devoid of political undertones. Other episodes in *Sogni d'oro* encourage us to identify Moretti with an even larger number of characters, sets of ideas and conflicts.

In *Sogni d'oro* Moretti constructs two distinct biographies: that of Michele Apicella and that of Sigmund Freud (or of a madman who believed that he was Freud). Freud is invoked in the film as the protagonist of Apicella's bio-pic, entitled *Freud's Mother*. In it, Apicella argues that the personality and the scientific achievements of Freud were the sole product of a dysfunctional upbringing. Hence, the father of psychoanalysis comes across as a hysterical and childish 'mama's boy' who invents psychoanalysis to come to terms with his own mental and emotional problems. It would seem that, by depicting the connection between one's childhood and his later life in a literal, simplistic way, and by portraying Freud as an old madman, Apicella ridicules the father of psychoanalysis; on the other hand, he seems to take his film's matter very seriously. It is in fact extremely difficult to distinguish Moretti's own position on psychoanalysis from that of his character Apicella – something that confirms the sophistication of Moretti's operation of disguise behind his alter ego.

The fact that Apicella, who suffers greatly due to his dependence on his mother (in one scene he even beats her up out of anger and frustration), chooses to make a film about a man whose mother also occupied a central position in his life, might result from his belief that by re-living, re-playing and re-viewing a life which was very much like his own he might be able to overcome his own problems. Such an attitude obviously belongs to the psychoanalytical discourse and it could be suggested that *Freud's Mother*, which is Michele's 'surrogate autobiography', is meant to fulfil a therapeutic function in the artist's life. The question arises whether he is successful; whether his film enables him to distance himself from his own mother, to become himself and find peace and happiness. The answer, if it appears in the film at all, is ambiguous. During the shooting of the film, Michele becomes increasingly neurotic and unhappy, in accordance with the theory that psychotherapy is always stressful and painful for the patient, because it brings suppressed traumas to the surface. In the end, he acquires a united personality, as his second, hidden soul comes out completely when Michele transforms into a werewolf. He even seems to accept his monstrosity, as suggested by his last words, directed to his beloved Silvia: 'Yes, I love you, I am a monster!' The werewolf is a symbol of schizophrenia; as Sir Talbot, the protagonist of Wagner's *The Wolf Man* (1940), observes of lycanthropy, 'like most legends it must have some basis in fact – it's probably an ancient explanation of the dual personality in most of us' (quoted in Tudor 1989: 99). A werewolf is also a very cinematographic object, almost a symbol of certain types of cinema (visionary, unrealistic); therefore, Michele's transformation might be regarded as a sign of his ultimate preference of cinema to life. In this sense, Michele's recovery remains problematic. The schizophrenic split experienced by Michele in *Sogni d'oro*, as well as being a repository of the anxieties of the real Moretti, could be read as symbolic of his own painful, schizophrenic predicament of being both the author (subject) and the protagonist (object) of his film.

The autobiographical discourse is particularly multi-layered in the last film in which Moretti plays Apicella: *Palombella rossa*. Here the director goes further towards convincing us of the autobiographical character of his work than in the earlier films, by including footage of the young Moretti, selling a left-wing publication door to door. The footage comes from his early Super-8 short *La sconfitta*, but the impression is that of watching a documentary about Apicella/Moretti, because the character is physically identical to the protagonist of two earlier Apicella films: *Io sono un autarchico* and *Ecce Bombo*. In two of his earlier films, *Sogni d'oro* and *Bianca*, Moretti included real photographs of himself. Primarily, these fulfil the function of images of Michele Apicella. However, due to the apparent authenticity of photography, they may also be perceived as photographs of the real Moretti and, as a result, enhance the autobiographical effect of these films. This is especially true of *Bianca*, where we clearly see a picture of Moretti at the age of about seven, amongst his peers at a school party.

Secondly, *Palombella rossa* touches on two major interests of the real Moretti: politics and water polo. Both passions, as with the cinema in the case of Apicella in *Sogni d'oro*, are a source of unease and even of suffering for the character. For example, in the flashback sequences, in which Apicella returns to his childhood, he is shown as having great doubts about his sporting career. We see him asking his mother to transfer him to a different sports class and musing in solitude how much easier it would be playing tennis or the piano. More importantly, the Communist Party, which Apicella joined when he was a teenager, and which he has represented in parliament for many years, is undergoing a deep crisis, in parallel with the real crisis experienced by PCI, the Italian Communist Party, at the time the film was made – again reinforcing the impression of realism and of autobiography.

An important factor in Michele's impotence is his amnesia, from which he has suffered since a car accident. It has made him detached from life, inward looking and day-dreaming, as epitomised by his fascination and identification with *Doctor Zhivago* (1965) by David Lean, a film often accused of trivialising the problems brought about by the October Revolution, and of changing it into Hollywood kitsch. Michele is neurotic and aggressive, as seen when he screams at and then slaps a journalist, as well as inadequate and impotent. His impotence is best revealed in a scene in which he is chosen by the manager to take the penalty that will decide the match, but he misses. The scene is repeated over and over again, on each occasion with the same, disappointing result (Michele does score once, but the referee had not whistled, thus the goal is disallowed). It appears as if Michele is unable to score because he thinks too much about how to shoot, instead of acting decisively and on instinct – which also might be read as a metaphor of PCI's inadequacies at the time. Again, as in *Sogni d'oro*, Michele Apicella is for the real Moretti a repository of his disappointments and anxieties, his inadequate version.

Palombella rossa is also important from the perspective applied in this chapter, in that this film not only presents a particular biography of Apicella/Moretti, but also deals with the theoretical issue of constructing biographies and identities. The film conveys the idea that biographies are not given to us once and for all, but that they are always constructed from the stories stored and reshaped in our memory and those narrated by our families and friends. The phrase 'Do you remember?' repeated in the film with obsessive frequency emphasises the importance of memory as a sculptor of people's biographies. Without memory, which is an active force, able to select and interpret, there is no biography and no identity. Consequently, there is never a definitive biography, biographies always change depending on who narrates them, for whom and when. Without stories about our lives (true or false), we would have no identity and, consequently, no life. In this respect, Moretti seems to agree with the previously mentioned opinion of Szymon Wrobel that a biography is always a cognitive achievement. Moretti conveys this concept through the previously mentioned device of making his protagonist amnesiac. At the beginning Michele does not remember anything and does not even know who he is; only through meetings with his friends, his family and people who know his public persona, and by gradually recollecting events from his past, often through dreams, he gets a sense of himself. His biography is woven of very heterogeneous material: trivia and things of the highest importance, images of himself (like the photograph on his team's membership that he carefully studies before the match), real and imaginary events, childhood memories and dreams, as well as recent occurrences. None of these 'testimonies' are completely reliable (for example, people whom he meets try to manipulate him), but ultimately they are the only material which Michele can use to create his biography and sense of self, and they are not very different from the fabric which all of us use to construct our identities – only that in Michele's case this material is obtained in a very short period of time.

Another issue, intrinsically connected with the production of biographies and present in *Palombella rossa*, is the problem of unity versus multiplicity of identities. In his book *Identity and the Life Cycle* (1994) Erik H. Erikson writes: 'The conscious feeling of having a *personal identity* is based on two simultaneous observations: the immediate perception of one's selfsameness and continuity in time; and the simultaneous perception of the fact that others recognise one's sameness and continuity' (1994: 22). If we accept this definition, then the personal identity of Apicella is presented as problematic, maybe even non-existent. The main cause of this disorder is the lack of continuity in time, caused both by Michele's amnesia and by the changes in his views and values which took place over the years. For example, Michele seems very ashamed of some things which he did in the past and cannot believe how they could have happened, in particular forcing a fellow pupil with fascist views to walk around with a sign around his neck. It feels as if Michele wants to disown this memory as if it belonged to somebody else. The misrecognition of one's own past selves is at work here.

In common with *Sogni d'oro*, *Palombella rossa* possesses a distinctive psycho-analytical stamp. For example, the division between memory and dream is blurred; memories are created by free association, which is reminiscent of Freud's concept of 'screen-memory': memory as dream and construction (Phillips 1994: 66). Furthermore, Moretti insists here on the importance of childhood in shaping one's adulthood and creating one's sense of self; the unresolved childhood traumas are clearly recognised as having the ability of affecting the decisions and general well-being of the adult individual.

Diary: authentic autobiography?

In discussing his roles in *Palombella rossa* and *Dear Diary*, Moretti stated:

> Perhaps I told a story about amnesia because I wanted to close the door on the character that I had played in my previous films, and start all over again with a new character that had to be completely constructed from scratch. This new character doesn't exist, because in *Dear Diary* I play myself and not a new character … In *Dear Diary*, it would have been absurd to hide myself behind a fictitious character because in the third part, *Doctors*, there's nothing that is invented. (Moretti in Porton & Ellickson 1995: 14)

The assertion that in *Dear Diary* Moretti plays himself, or even *is* himself, was repeated by the director in several more interviews given after the film's premiere, and was seized on by many critics, who – like Moretti himself – based this conclusion mainly on the fact that the protagonist's name is Nanni and that the film's third section contains some documentary material, shot in 16mm during the film-maker's own chemotherapy treatment. For these critics, these sequences somehow conferred documentary quality on the whole film. For example, Peter Aspden maintains: '[Moretti's] previous work has always contained autobiographical undertones, but this time he has gone all the way' (Aspden 1994: 42); for Paola Malanga the third episode of *Dear Diary* is 'pure autobiography' (Malanga 1993: 25); and according to Emanuela Martini *Dear Diary* is 'exclusively autobiographical' (Martini 1993: 59). Millicent Marcus writes:

> Having presented his brief documentary sequence, Moretti tells the rest of the story in flashback, simulating the rounds of medical visits and providing narrative continuity in voice-over. But the fact that we witnessed the chemotherapy session in newsreel form confers authority and gravity on the subsequent performance, for the body we see on screen is the same body that went through the ordeal to which we bore documentary witness – the mimetic body carries the traces of the mortal struggle being replayed before us. Like Dante who had to undergo the experience of Christian death and rebirth in order to be able to tell us his story, Moretti returns from chemotherapy to convey to us the mortal truth of his own particular human condition. (Marcus 1996: 244)

Only a minority of critics questioned the 'authenticity' of Moretti's account of his life and persona in *Dear Diary*. For example, Federica Villa draws attention to the fact that the film opens and closes with two 'unrealistic' shots, respectively a subjective shot and a look into the camera lens. She argues that, in particular, the last image of the film breaks the kind of 'pact' with the audience necessary for us to believe that we have been observing a diary. If this was pure autobiography, i.e. the following/shadowing of Moretti's life, the illusion that we are watching him living his own life should be sustained until the end, whereas that look into the lens and smile at the spectator breaks the illusion (cf. Villa 1999).

Both those who support and those who are critical of the opinion that *Dear Diary* is true autobiography (or a film which is as close to this ideal as possible) base their opinions on the characteristics of certain fragments of the film, as well as on exclusively formal aspects, ignoring other fragments and other features. Analogous arguments in favour and against the autobiographical character of Moretti's work can be formulated with reference to *Aprile*, which is the second film with 'Nanni Moretti' as the main character. For example, the fact that the director includes in *Aprile* sequences shot in his own home, in which members of his family participate, adds to the impression that we are watching Moretti's own life. On the other hand, the humorous nature of many intimate scenes, such as the pregnancy of Moretti's partner, the birth of his child and Moretti's use of psycho-babble when addressing his son, suggests that the director keeps a certain distance from the events depicted. Such a distance is very difficult to achieve in real life, particularly in poignant moments such as the birth of one's child. In addition, there are some significant disparities between what Moretti says in *Aprile* and what he shows; for instance, he claims that he will discourage his son from becoming an actor, but at the same time 'casts' little Pietro in one of the main parts of his film.

Our opinion as to the autobiographical character of these two films follows the general stance adopted in this chapter: complete or pure autobiographies are impossible, we can only talk about 'autobiographical effect' and analyse the means through which such effect is achieved. In *Dear Diary* and *Aprile* the principal vehicle to accomplish the autobiographical effect is the use of what is presented as the author's diary.

The diary is widely assumed to be the form of artistic expression that is most faithful to its author. Thomas Mallon argues: 'One can read a poem or a novel without coming to know its author, look at a painting and fail to get a sense of its painter; but one cannot read a diary and feel unacquainted with its writer. No form of expression more emphatically embodies the expresser: diaries are the flesh made word' (Mallon 1984: xvii). Mallon defines a diary as 'carrier of the private, the everyday, the intriguing, the sordid, the sublime, the boring – in short, a chronicle of everything' (1984: 1). The diary is often described as a para-literary form, rather than pure literature, because it is assumed that, in contrast to a novel or a poem, which demand considerable talent, anybody can write a diary. As Mallon puts it, 'Diary-writing is the poor man's art' (1984: xiii). This opinion excludes the possibility of distinguishing between 'poor man's diaries', that is, diaries that are purely private, and diaries that contain ideas of wider importance and appeal. Many diaries reached the status of art, for instance the diary of Samuel Pepys, which for centuries was the model of this form of writing.

It is only in recent decades that the notion of diary-making has extended beyond the traditional, written form and, consequently, that the boundaries between the diary and other forms of art became blurred. The term 'diary' is now often applied to works which are mainly or even purely visual, for example photographs by Christian Boltanski and Darren Almond, Emma Kay's and Jeremy Deller's maps made from memory, paintings by John Baldessari, applique quilts and video productions by Tracey Emin. The term 'diary' may also be used with reference to the work of some film directors, such as Andy Warhol, Derek Jarman, Stan Brakhage and Patrick Keiller. Although these film-makers are all regarded as radical representatives of modernist/postmodernist art and cinema, their films are very different in their style and content, testifying to the immense scope of 'diary' to accommodate various artistic interests and temperaments.

The diary has recently gained the status of the epitome of art: the opinion that every artist's body of art is ultimately his/her diary is now often expressed. 'Diary', the exhibition held in 1999 at the Cornerhouse gallery in Manchester and devoted to artists who use a diary as their principal form of artistic expression, was meant to illustrate and demonstrate the changes in the diary discourse in contemporary art. In the exhibition's catalogue Margot Heller argues:

> Art, like a diary, is inherently individual, in a sense representing the artist's thoughts at particular moments in time. Most works of art are given a date to register the significance of the time when they were made, and the majority of retrospective shows are organised chronologically, inviting us to witness the different stages of artists' lives unfurl as revealed through the development of their work. Art can thus be a metaphor for a diary. (Heller 1999: 113)

For those who are lonely, 'a diary can provide a channel through which to converse with oneself, transforming monologue into dialogue with the ever-receptive diary becoming the tireless companion and confidant, and an antidote to loneliness' (Heller 1999: 118). For those who are very busy and involved in many different projects at a time, writing a diary is a way to preserve one's identity, to give coherence to one's fragmented existence. It is not surprising that psychiatrists advise their patients to keep a diary as a way of maintaining or improving their mental health. It is also widely accepted that in these times of 'liquid modernity', to use Zygmunt Bauman's expression, marked by schizophrenia and by the end of meta-narratives, it is more difficult than in any earlier epoch both to furnish one's identity with unity and coherence and to create any scientific, philosophical or artistic synthesis or 'summa'. Consequently, a diary, in its shameless and unapologetic affirmation of multitude and equality of discourses in private lives and in culture and, at the same time, in its ability to set in order (however minimal this order may be) the magma of individual and collective experience, appears to be the perfect tool for recognising and overcoming the discursive disorder affecting individuals and societies. The affinity of the diary form to postmodern art lies also in its openness; a diary, unlike a novel or a poem, at least in principle, does not need to be concluded. The only compulsory end to a diary is the author's death.

Diaries also, as Margot Heller suggests, 'sharpen our consciousness of time and whether we are mapping out next week's appointments, planning our social life or even secretly recording memories of the recent past, diaries force us to see things in terms of a timescale. If there is one defining trait shared by all diaries ... it is the significance of time, no matter how discretely conveyed, as a framework against which to chart experience' (Heller 1999: 114).

All the aforementioned reasons for writing a diary and for producing art in the form of a diary – to sharpen one's consciousness of time, to be personal and to convey the multitude and equality of discourses – can be attributed to Moretti. Accordingly time, both objective and subjective, or to use Proust's phrase 'regained' and transformed by memory, plays a crucial role in *Dear Diary* and in *Aprile*, although in these two films Moretti employs and elucidates different temporal characteristics. In *Dear Diary* the director focuses on the passage of time in his private life as well as in Italy's history. Hence, in the first 'chapter', 'On my Vespa', we see him pondering how Rome's architecture and quality of life has changed since the 1960s. His general impression is one of decline. In the second chapter, 'Islands', Moretti shows how Stromboli, which in the famous film by Rossellini (1950) epitomised the danger and awe of nature as well as the traditionalism and simplicity of Italian folk, became a near-simulacrum: a destination for American visitors, who regard the menacing volcano merely as a tourist attraction. Moretti also refers to events which are as much a part of the history of modern Italy as of Moretti's own life, such as the murder of Pier Paolo Pasolini in 1975. Moretti's sifting through newspaper clippings from the time of Pasolini's murder and his subsequent visit to the scene of his death, where an abominable monument shows signs of ageing, make the passage of time tangible. Moretti also points to the shame of a death that nobody wants to remember, hence by literally and metaphorically re-visiting Pasolini's murder, he draws our attention to the importance of remembering: without memory there would be no history, no individual or collective past. Thus, a role of the diary is to be the repository of memory for both the writer and the reader.

In *Aprile* the emphasis is not so much on things already passed and transformed by memory, but on catching a particular moment in time, on the making of individual and social history. The director concentrates on two events: the victory of Berlusconi in the 1994 parliamentary elections and the birth of his son, Pietro. Although these events belong to different spheres, they are both at great risk of being forgotten or misrepresented, if not immediately recorded: children grow so fast that their parents never believe how small they once were; political discourse, especially in Italy, is very 'fluid' – politicians tend to deny what they said even a short time earlier.

If a diary, more than any other form of artistic expression, furnishes the work of art with personal character, then it is open to the same objections and has similar potential advantages as 'ordinary' autobiography. Hence, the detractors of artistic diaries might point out that using the diary form, as opposed to making a 'normal' novel or film, testifies to the artist's egotism and narcissism, to his conviction of his greatness and importance, to his belief that the audience is interested in everything he produces, irrespective of its quality. Supporters of diaries would instead argue that the artist-diarist is the paragon of a modest, humble artist who does not presume to describe the whole world or, indeed, anything beyond what is experienced by him here and now. Off-screen Moretti wants us to believe that he belongs to a group of 'humble diarists' when he confesses in an interview: 'It is not because of conceit that I said that I would like to make films about myself. It was simply the only thing I was able to do. And it somehow happened that, when I talked about myself, I also talked about other people' (Osmolska-Metrak 1994: 19).

In foregrounding the desire to be completely sincere with the audience, as well as to capture a particular moment of time in his films, Moretti is reminiscent of a fellow Italian film-maker: Cesare Zavattini. Zavattini (who also often privileged the diary form in his literary works) claimed that to write and to film in the first person offered him the opportunity to be immediate and sincere: 'We should not talk on behalf of others, but in the name of ourselves ... For this reason I believe that it is actually necessary to be autobiographical, that it is necessary to use the first person' (Zavattini in Fortichiari 1992: 66). This perfectly suits the position taken by Moretti in *Dear Diary* and *Aprile*.[4]

In *Dear Diary* and *Aprile* Moretti presents himself to us as a humble artist and an ordinary man. In *Dear Diary* his position is in no way privileged or superior to that of the other characters. On the contrary, he usually represents himself as inferior to them. Take the case of 'On my Vespa', which chronicles Moretti's travelling through Rome, deserted due to the summer holidays. His trip is largely made up of his participation in cultural and artistic events. However, contrary to what one might expect, Moretti does not put himself forward as an art producer, but as its consumer, moreover one who is rather unsophisticated. With an eagerness more easily associated with a teenage fan than with a famous Italian film *auteur*, he confesses that Adrian Lyne's *Flashdance* (1983) changed his life and learning to dance became one of the greatest dreams of his life. He meets, as if by chance, *Flashdance* star Jennifer Beals, who is strolling with her director husband, Alexander Rockwell, and repeats to her his confession about his love of the film and of the art of dancing. The American couple treat his revelation with amusement, and Moretti himself with suspicion. In a short conversation in English which Moretti only half-understands, they describe him as 'off-centre' and 'almost dumb'. It is suggested that they fail to recognise him as a famous Italian director; for them, he is only one more obsessed fan and they pass him by without further discussion. Humility is also revealed in the scene at the place of Pasolini's murder, which Nanni visits as an ordinary admirer, not as a fellow director.

Another situation in which we see Moretti as a consumer of art is when he goes to the cinema to see *Henry: Portrait of a Serial Killer* (1986) by John McNaughton. Later, Moretti imagines being at the bedside of a critic who wrote an enthusiastic review of this film, and punishing him by forcing him to listen to his absurd prose. While watching the film, as well as during his 'punishment' of the critic, Moretti assumes the rather modest position of an ordinary, perhaps even old-fashioned viewer and reader, who rejects violence on screen and does not understand the postmodern jargon used by Italian journalists. In *Dear Diary* Nanni is also represented as humble in the material sense: his Vespa looks very modest and fragile against the background of the cars which he passes on his journey. Moreover, when he visits the fashionable and historic quarter of Garbatella he finds out that he cannot afford to buy any of the beautiful penthouses. The only time when he confesses to someone that he is a film-maker, his suggestion that he wants to shoot a musical set in the 1950s about a Trotskyite pastry cook is so absurd that we find it difficult to imagine him being taken seriously.

Moretti's ordinariness and humility is best conveyed in the third part of *Dear Diary*, 'Doctors', in which the director depicts his experience of having Hodgkin's disease, a form of cancer. As has already been mentioned, the majority of critics were struck by the documentary feel of this part, and the autobiographical status of *Dear Diary* is based mainly upon the theme and style of 'Doctors'. We will suggest that this impression of authenticity is, to a great extent, the result of Moretti's deviation from the illness discourse typically found in the history of art. While art historians tend to romanticise the artist's illness, and closely connect it with the high-quality and dramatic character of the artist's production, Moretti, by contrast, offers us a portrayal of illness taken entirely out of artistic context. His cancer is a completely overpowering and debilitating condition which renders him unable to sleep or concentrate on anything apart from an awful itching, which is wrongly diagnosed by successive doctors as a symptom of a skin disease or of a food allergy. It is clear that making films, or indeed any other form of productive activity, was out of the question for Moretti at the time of his illness. His whole social life is represented as reduced to visiting doctors, chemists and other people offering him medical advice, in common with the lives of many other sick people which 'shrink' once they are overwhelmed by suffering. The only friends mentioned by Nanni in 'Doctors' are an immunologist and someone who arranges an appointment for him with a famous dermatologist. Moretti's mother is referred to as the one who gave him silk pyjamas to alleviate the itching and his partner, Silvia, only appears once with him and this is in a hospital waiting room. Moreover, the illness makes the character aware of his ultimate weakness and dependence on others, as in the scene in which one of the dermatologists visited by Moretti tells him that 'You act like a loser. It is psychological. It depends on you', thus suggesting that he should overcome the illness by himself. 'If it depends on me,' says the protagonist on his way home, 'I'm sure I won't make it.'

On the whole, his is the illness of an ordinary man and, to use the famous phrase of Susan Sontag, 'without a metaphor' – a condition which

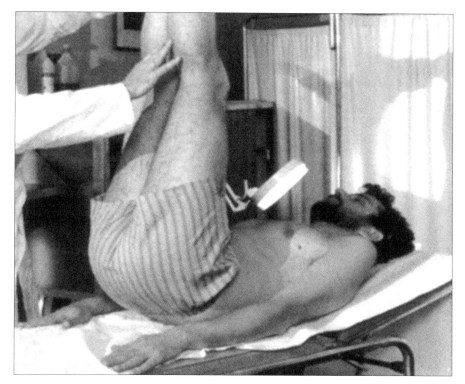

Nanni during a medical examination in 'Doctors' (*Dear Diary*, 1994)

does not mean anything apart from itself. Sontag herself regards this as the proper way to treat illness. She writes: 'My point is that illness is *not* a metaphor – and the healthiest way of being ill is one most purified of, most resistant to, metaphoric thinking' (Sontag 1979: 3). Paradoxically, the very act of making 'Doctors' is testimony to the claim that illness helps artistic creativity – cancer helped Moretti to make one of his best films, a work which is exceptional in its simplicity and power.

The fact that the episode's protagonist is an artist who is ill with cancer encourages us to compare 'Doctors' with other films on this subject, and particularly with *The Belly of an Architect* (1987) by Peter Greenaway, a film-maker who, in common with Moretti, has been labelled a postmodernist. This comparison shows why Moretti, as represented in 'Doctors', seems such an ordinary man. As the title suggests, Greenaway's artist, an architect named Stourley Kracklite, suffers from stomach cancer which, as in Moretti's case, is wrongly diagnosed at first – this time as dyspepsia. Both artists try to document their illness, the architect by making pictures of his own belly and of bellies similar to his, Moretti by collecting prescriptions for medicines and by making a film about his chemotherapy sessions. Yet the differences are more important than the similarities. In particular, Greenaway misleads everybody, including the audience, about his protagonist's true condition. Kracklite is not only unsure of the cause of his stomach pain, but he hardly wants to find out. Unlike Moretti, he visits the doctor very late in the day and seems not to mind much when the diagnosis does not suit his own opinion of his condition. Moreover, he ultimately proves to be unwilling to be cured, or he does not believe that his condition can be helped, and commits suicide. Furthermore, in Greenaway's film, unlike in Moretti's, the illness is used primarily as a metaphor, or even as a multi-functional metaphor for what is felt to be socially or morally wrong. Kracklite's large belly is constantly compared with the bellies of Roman statues and changed into artistic 'representation': a photograph, a copy of its photograph, a copy of the copy, and so on. On many occasions, Greenaway suggests that both the ancient Roman society and the contemporary Western world are characterised by excessive consumption and corruption. It almost feels as if cancer is a kind of punishment for Kracklite's overindulgence in food and drink, for having too large a belly. According to Sontag, 'Cancer is a disease of middle-class life, a disease associated with affluence, with excess' (Sontag 1979: 15) and this perfectly fits Greenaway's diagnosis of his protagonist. By contrast, Moretti avoids any associations between his cancer and the state of society at large. In particular, by revealing the ignorance and arrogance of the doctor who regards his illness as a psychological condition, even as a kind of punishment, he criticises the notion of illness as a retribution for some mental/psychological deficiency, a suggestion which, as Sontag observes, often obscures the doctors' helplessness in establishing the true cause of a disease. Moretti's approach is clearly not only more scientific and rational, but also more 'patient-friendly', as it removes from the sufferer the burden of guilt. Ultimately, it is also more optimistic as, in spite of the ignorance of many doctors, his search for a cure in the end was rewarded, and he regained his health.

'Doctors' perfectly conforms to the claim that a diary is the most personal form of art. A diary also proves to be a perfect tool for reconciling the two functions of art: the personal and the public. Thomas Mallon observes:

Artists' diaries often hesitate and shift between the personal and the professional. In some of them notes for projects are crowded by reports on romance and weather ... Just as the distinction between *journal* and *diary* eludes clarification, the point at which a diary becomes a notebook, and vice versa, is difficult to locate. (Mallon 1984: 119–20)

This is also the case of *Dear Diary*: in spite of its apparently light and strictly personal character, in it Moretti tries to reconcile his role as a private diarist with that of critic and 'soul of the nation'. For example, the second part of the film, 'Islands', can be read as a metaphor of the heterogeneity and fragmentation of Italian society. As Moretti himself claimed in an interview, his purpose was to demonstrate that the islands 'do not communicate', they live separate, disconnected, introverted lives (cf. Porton & Ellickson 1995: 15). Being 'the poor man's art', art without any presumption of authority, the diary is an excellent vehicle to convey one of the film's main ideas: the crisis of authority (a theme present in many of Moretti's films, including *La messa è finita* and *Palombella rossa*) or perhaps the superfluity of authority. These issues are developed in 'Islands', when Gerardo, a dedicated Joyce scholar, changes during a short trip into a television addict, whose favourite programmes become those most lacking in intellectual ambition: soap operas and quiz shows. To an even larger extent, the crisis of authority is addressed in 'Doctors', where those whom society entrust more than the members of most other professions prove to be completely incompetent. In the last scene of the film, in which the protagonist reveals what he learnt during his illness, he says: 'Doctors know how to talk, but not how to listen.' It could be argued that Moretti's own film is built on the opposite premise – listening and suspending judgment, rather than imposing on the viewers ready-made recipes and simple conclusions.

In common with *Dear Diary*, the use of the diary in *Aprile* furnishes the film with personal character and allows the author to represent both his private and public existence without any rupture in the content and style of the film. As mentioned previously, *Aprile* shows the life of Moretti's son from the first months of the pregnancy to when Pietro is about one year old, and also deals with two general elections in Italy, one of which Nanni tries to depict through a documentary. At the same time, he (not unlike the protagonist of the first part of *Dear Diary*) dreams of making a musical about a Trotskyite pastry cook set in the 1950s. Hence, in *Aprile* Moretti shows us how multifaceted, heterogeneous, intense and hectic is his existence. This impression is much stronger than in *Dear Diary*, where Moretti makes only tacit reference to his film-making career and where many aspects of his life are overlooked.

Once again the protagonist is made to look humble. In his private life Nanni comes across as an awkward, almost inadequate 'new man' who tries to support the mother of his child during all the stages of her pregnancy and birth, and to share equally the duties of bringing up a child, but does not quite manage. Moretti also reveals his problems and inadequacies in his life as a film-maker. Being a committed socialist, he feels that it is his duty to make a documentary that will reveal the state in which Italy finds itself, and everybody whom he meets is of the same opinion. At the same time, he has serious doubts about his right and ability to make it. For example, on his way to a location he confesses to his collaborators: 'I'm not trying to convince anyone. I want to say what I think. But how can I say what I think in a documentary? And what do I think exactly?' The protagonist's difficulty with engaging in politics and making a documentary about Italy also results from his preoccupation with his domestic life and his young son. Every time he is supposed to film an important political event or interview a politician, he prefers to shoot little Pietro or simply cannot concentrate on his work, because his mind is somewhere else. Once again, the diary proves to be the perfect tool both to reveal the tensions and conflicts caused by juggling private/family duties and professional/political duties (one of the main problems of modern life), and a vehicle to overcome them.

The impression of Moretti's humility also derives from the fact that, as Chris Wagstaff observes, the film's protagonist questions his adulthood:

One of the main themes of the film is the opposition between infantilism and adulthood: the birth of a son raises the question for Nanni of when and even whether, he should become an adult. A friend gives him a tape-measure for his birthday, and shows him how much time he has left (if he plans on living to 80) in terms of length of tape. Nanni decides he will live to 95, putting off adulthood for the time being ... Nanni's job is making films, but he cannot choose between the public, responsible, adult documentary on the political state of contemporary Italy, and the private, infantile fantasy of a musical about a Roman pastry cook. (Wagstaff 1999: 36)

His unwillingness to grow up can give the impression that Nanni in *Aprile* is very much like Michele in films such as *Sogni d'oro* and *Palombella rossa*. Yet there is also a significant difference between the types of infantilism conveyed in *Aprile* and in the Apicella films respectively. For Michele, not being able to grow up was a source of trauma as well as an obstacle to leading an independent, adult life and to having a family of his own. In *Aprile*, on the contrary, a dose of childishness seems to be an advantage in being a happy father and a happy man.

While Moretti as the protagonist of *Aprile* fails to make a documentary about contemporary Italy (and it is not clear if he will succeed in completing his musical), Moretti as the author of *Aprile* succeeds in giving us a rich insight into 1990s Italy, with its unstable politics, the Berlusconi phenomenon, the advance of the Northern League, the growing indifference of politicians of all sides towards immigrants, and the deplorable state of the Italian media. Moreover, in spite of the apparently personal, casual, even humorous attitude towards most of the problems represented, and despite being interspersed with stories from the protagonist's private life, the moral tone of *Aprile* is not neutral. Ultimately, we know what Moretti thinks and on whose side he wants us to be – the side of the political left, but a left which is strong, united, idealistic and self-critical. A large part of the author's subtle, but effective, proselytising work is done by strictly filmic means; for example, as Wagstaff observes, 'the episode of Umberto Bossi's declaration of the independence of Padania is filmed with ironical grandeur' (Wagstaff 1999: 36).

Moretti's vulnerability to humiliation, his irony and self-irony and even shame at his words and deeds, his constant questioning of his moral and political stance, his desire to make personal, eccentric films, and also to use cinema as a political weapon for the left, and his unwillingness to mature, as presented in *Dear Diary* and *Aprile*, make his moral stance reminiscent of the previously quoted Richard Rorty. Two features of Rorty's thought seem to be particularly close to Moretti's outlook on life: his concise formula that a person is somebody prone to humiliation (therefore solidarity must play a crucial role in human relations), and his conviction that there is no 'final dictionary', no ultimate description of the world, and that therefore one should not take oneself too seriously – which is the core of Rorty's theory of 'irony'.[5]

Conclusion: from Apicella to Moretti

Given that pure and complete autobiography is impossible to achieve, for all the reasons expounded in the introductory section of this chapter, we disagree with those critics who look at Moretti's cinema as his true life story. Moretti's greatest artistic achievement in fact is, in our opinion, the creation of a sophisticated 'fictional autobiography', or even of a fiction that looks like a documentary on the life of citizen Nanni Moretti. The 'autobiographical effect' is reached through visual, narrative and stylistic means, such as the complex game of recurrence and variation of traits in his alter ego in the Apicella films, and the adoption of the form of the diary in *Dear Diary* and *Aprile*.

In conclusion, whereas the autobiographical effect is present in all of Moretti's films, it is stronger in those whose main character is Nanni, in comparison with those who feature Michele Apicella. At the same time, we can observe a shift in the development of Moretti's protagonist towards reconciliation with his own shortcomings and with the world at large. This impression gains strength if we compare the endings of the films belonging to the two respective groups. Whereas the Apicella films finish with the character being defeated, or at best confused, as well as angry and disappointed with the world, the endings of the Moretti films send a much more positive message about politics, cinema, life and Nanni's place in the world. It feels as if the character has mellowed over the years, without losing his ability to see the world in 'sharp focus', without abandoning his critical and ironic edge. Such an opinion was expressed by critics and the director alike. For example, when comparing his earlier films with *Dear Diary*, Moretti said: 'I always collect newspapers clippings, but rarely look at them. It is also true that so far I collected mainly negative information and this was visible in my films, which denounced the cinema which I disliked. In *Dear Diary*, by contrast – and the audience probably senses it – I wanted to express my affirmation of the type of cinema which I like to do' (Osmolska-Metrak 1994: 19–20). Discussing the same film, Peter Aspden claims: 'When Moretti smiles to the camera at the end of his ordeal and downs his daily glass of water, life is being affirmed in the most modest, and effective, of ways' (Aspden 1994: 43). Even more joy of life can be detected in the ending of *Aprile*, in which the character, dressed in a rather eccentric winter cape (which previously he hadn't the courage to wear), first gets rid of the numerous newspaper clippings which he collected for twenty years solely because they made him angry, and then goes to the studio where the shooting of his long-dreamt film about the pastry cook begins. This episode presents an ideal way of dealing with one's past: to purge oneself of the poisonous relics of the past and make real that which was only a 'sweet dream'.

We could risk saying that the bridging of the gap between the film's author and his protagonist by openly admitting that they are the same person is what saved Nanni in the diary films from the schizophrenia experienced by Michele in many of the Apicella films. However, it must be stressed that the protagonist's success in *Dear Diary* and *Aprile* in dealing with himself and the world was hard fought, and that the phase of being Apicella probably played a major role in his victory.

CHAPTER TWO

Viva la famiglia!: Individuals, Families and the Crisis of Masculinity

One has to leave home one day. Maybe the sooner the better.
– David Cooper

I do not want to overcome my Oedipus!
– Michele Apicella

In the previous chapter we argued that, from the perspective of the use of autobiography, Moretti's films should be divided into a number of groups. A similar categorisation also proves useful in treating Moretti's exploration of issues concerning the family and, specifically, the relationship between the individual (particularly a male individual) and the family – issues which will be the focus of this chapter. There are two main reasons for dividing Moretti's films into groups here: the shift in the representation of the male subject and of the family that took place in the course of Moretti's oeuvre; and the impression that in successive films Moretti represents the same character at different stages of his life. Consequently, we have divided the films into three groups: the first comprises films about a young man who rejects his family ties and commitments and who either becomes 'autarchic' or joins a commune or other alternative group; the second represents an older character who seeks a perfect family, but abstains from beginning one; the third group is about 'real', as opposed to 'ideal' families, and a man who eventually establishes his own family.

Italian families in the 1980s and 1990s

In order to understand Moretti's representation of families and of the individual's relationship with this ancient institution, as well as the importance or even centrality of the discourse on family in his work, we will situate his cinema within the context of the recent social history of Italy. Paul Ginsborg, in his books *A History of Contemporary Italy* and *Italy and Its Discontents*, which cover the entire post-war history of this country, draws attention to two features that characterised Italian families in the 1980s and 1990s. The first is their cohesiveness, stability, continuity and strength. For example, Ginsborg quotes a survey of Italy undertaken by *The Economist* in May 1990 which proclaims family to be 'the enduring unit of Italian society. It explains the lack of public spirit in Italy, and even of the concept of public good … It explains the Mafia, the biggest family of them all. It also explains the pattern of business. From the Agnelli down, Italians like to keep control of their affairs within the family' (Ginsborg 2001: 68).

Statistical data support this claim. For example, the divorce rate in Italy is low in relation to that of the rest of the Western world. In 1980, six years after divorce was introduced, the number of divorces in Italy was 11,800, that is, 0.2 per 1,000 inhabitants. Today Italy is, together with Ireland, the country in Europe with the lowest number of divorces, 0.7 per 1,000 inhabitants, against a European average of 1.9 (Gallo 2001: 15). In the 1980s and 1990s there was also a relatively low number of lone parent families and of births outside marriage as a percentage of total births in Italy. In 1980 only 4.3 per cent of children were born outside marriage, a figure that grew to 9.6 in the year 2000, but that is still very low when compared with the European average of 28.4 per cent (ibid.). Moreover, inter-generational solidarity in Italy is greater than in the rest of Western Europe: 'Grandparents, parents and children often live close together and in daily contact with one another'

(Ginsborg 2001: 74). Therefore, Ginsborg describes Italian families as 'long'. They are also characterised by 'frequent contacts between members of the extended family, especially cousins. All this caused Italian families to express particular qualities of spatial and emotional proximity' (ibid.).

The second main characteristic of the contemporary Italian family is that of being 'thin', as a result of the extremely low fertility rate of Italian women. From having one of the highest birth rates in Europe, Italy now has the lowest in the whole Western world. From the peak year of 1964, when 1,032,000 babies were born, the rate has declined to 552,000 in 1987 (Ginsborg 1987: 414). In 1970, the average number of children per woman in Italy was 2.42 (around the norm for the European community), by 1980 it was 1.64, by 1990 1.3, and by 1993 1.21 (Ginsborg 2001: 69). In the year 2000, the birth rate was 1.24, against a European average of 1.47 (Gallo 2001: 15). Ginsborg put forward two main contributory factors for this low birth rate. The first was, paradoxically, not the emancipation of Italian women, but its incomplete nature, which led to a self-imposed restraint.

> Italian women may still have wanted two children, but the pressures of their lives made such symmetry difficult to obtain. Men still did too little to help at home; the principal tasks of caring fell upon the mother of each family; working women found themselves drained by their 'double presence', in their homes and in their jobs. As the new liberty of individual choice and the use of some measure of contraception spread from elites and permeated Italian families, women's vision of themselves changed. This subjective transformation ... told against the choice for a second or even a third child. (Ginsborg 2001: 72)

The second reason, 'an exasperated neo-Malthusian prudence' on the part of Italian parents and of women in particular, was the previously mentioned prospect of having to care for older members of the family: 'Here was a second paradox: it was the very strength of the Italian family that contributed to its numerical diminution' (ibid.).

The fact of being 'thin and long' has significant implications for the internal dynamics of Italian families. One of them is a particularly strong, but not always healthy relationship between mothers and sons, who on average remain in the parental home longer than their sisters. Secondly, the dominant model of a family with only one child, one who was often born when the parents were over thirty, made the children the object of an unhealthy hyper-attention and hyper-affection on the part of their parents and grandparents, delaying the process of the child's emancipation and largely infantilising Italian families (Ginsborg 2001: 80). One of the most extreme and humorous examples of these trends was reported by the Italian and international press in April 2002, and inspired a French film by Étienne Chatiliez (*Tanguy*, 2001). This was a court maintenance battle between a father and his adult son. The loser in this argument, Giuseppe Andreoli, is an anatomy professor and a former member of parliament, who refused to financially support his thirty-year-old son, Marco Andreoli, a graduate in Law still living with his mother. The court, however, ruled that Giuseppe Andreoli must continue to pay Marco around £500 per month until he can find himself satisfactory employment. Italian commentators warned that 'the decision could depress Italy's already low birth rate and discourage people from leaving home, getting married and having children' (Willan 2002: 2).

We will argue that Moretti's films illustrate and comment on many of these trends that have been present in Italian family life over the last twenty years. In his family portraits, the film-maker often uses derision, but also self-irony, since he himself lived with his parents until he was 29. As he confessed in 1987:

> Four years ago I moved out of my parents' apartment – a bit late indeed, I was 29, which is the regional record in Lazio, nobody leaves his or her parents that late – and when I made *Bianca* and *La messa è finita*, during the phase of the shooting, since I did not feel like living on my own, I went back to stay with my parents. (Gili 1987: 16)

Looking for alternatives to a nuclear family

Io sono un autarchico was widely interpreted by the critics and by the audience alike as the manifesto of a young director who proclaims his independence of and distance from the Italian cinema of that time; in fact the word of Greek origin 'autarchic' used in the title can be translated as 'self-sufficient'. Although such an interpretation accurately captures Moretti's position in the panorama of national cinema after the premiere of *Io sono un autarchico*, it hardly reflects the actual subject of the film. Its protagonist, Michele Apicella, is not a film-maker so he cannot be autarchic as described above.

The term 'autarchic' refers instead to his personal situation. Moretti himself confirmed this reading: 'By *autarchia* I understood here the emotional and sexual situation of the character who, having been left by his wife, must look after his young son. He is a kind of a boy/father. My film also contains a scene of masturbation and the title acknowledges this aspect of his life' (Osmolska-Metrak 1994: 18). This short description, although correct, does not explain the aetiology or consequences of the character's situation, nor does it reveal the director's attitude to being emotionally and sexually 'autarchic'. For that, we must turn to the film's text.

Although Moretti in *Io sono un autarchico*, in common with his later films, avoids detailed explanations of his characters' actions, the marital separation with which the film opens is principally attributed to the young mother's sense of confinement and loss of autonomy in the family. Moretti presents both parents as incapable of accepting responsibility: Michele says that, since he has to finish university (even though we never see him studying), he cannot support the family; Silvia complains that she does not have time to read or to have her own life. A second reason for the break-up is the lack of harmony between the two, who maintain that they cannot even remember why they got married. The young parents are presented as a typical post-1968 couple who, in the open and liberal climate of the youth revolution, lived a spontaneous romantic and sexual experience, but then found it impossible to adapt to their new parenting role. As often in Italian films that examine this topic, examples of which are Peter Del Monte's *Piso Pisello* (1981) and Francesca Archibugi's *Verso sera* (*Towards Evening*, 1990) and *L'albero delle pere* (*The Pear Tree*, 1998), the post-1968 mother and father are depicted as selfish and absent, while the children, usually depicted as more mature than their parents, are either left to themselves or handed over to their grandparents. In the case of *Io sono un autarchico*, it is the father who assumes responsibility, while the mother leaves the family home. Little Andrea is shown throughout the film as a serious and detached child, who plays mainly on his own, favouring solipsistic games of cards. Somehow, his father looks more childish than him. Through the scene of the break-up, Moretti straight away describes his protagonist as being very immature, certainly more so than his wife – whereas she has demonstrated courage through her actions, and possibly her complaints are more justified (the film never states it clearly, but she could well have been the family's breadwinner up to now), he hides behind his nagging sense of humour (he pretends he does not remember how old she is, and tells her that she speaks like the characters in an American film of forty years ago), and instead of expressing his pain and anger at being left, he uses small Andrea to try and persuade her to stay. Only when it is clear that his strategy is not going to work, Michele breaks down and begins to cry childishly.

Michele's attitude to his wife seems to suggest that he barely recognises a woman's right to equality in family life. He is in fact very demanding towards her, while apparently being unaware of his responsibility in the failure of their marriage. On the other hand, his behaviour in the aftermath of the separation shows that he has absorbed progressive ideas relating to family life and the organisation of society. The most obvious sign is the fact that Andrea remains with him. Moretti does not explain whether the arrangement followed a mutual agreement, or resulted from the mother's or from the father's insistence. Towards the end of the film, the son is returned to his mother, again for reasons not conveyed to the viewers. However, the very fact that in this household bringing up children is not treated exclusively as a mother's duty is meaningful, suggesting that Michele has at least partially internalised the 'new man' ethos. In his relationship with his son, the protagonist usually proves to be tender and friendly, but he is also a rather clumsy father, behaving more like an older brother than a father, as Moretti himself acknowledged in interviews. Michele involves Andrea in his own interests: he takes him to the rehearsals of the independent theatre production in which he takes part, where the little boy is treated by his father's friends as one of the performers. At other times Michele plays with Andrea, has breakfast and dinner with him, and once we see him taking him to school. When confronted with daily but challenging tasks such as convincing little Andrea to eat or go to sleep, his impotence (but also his self-irony, given the exaggeration of these scenes) is revealed by his attempts at parental methods that are typical of an older generation, for instance threatening his child or trying to fool him. On one occasion, Michele's frustration in his paternal role is revealed by his thoughts as expressed in voice-over: 'Why do I have this clear desire to strangle you?' Overall, Michele is rather successful as a father, even if his behaviour is often more childish than his child's.

After Silvia has left, Michele is unable to detach himself from her and from their common past, but neither can he express his feelings for his wife. He keeps phoning her, but then remains silent, or says generic phrases, while his distress is evident from his facial expressions. He meets her several times to talk, but continues to nag her rather than try to win her back. Once he refuses to give her back Andrea, protesting that if he stayed with his mother by the age of twelve or thirteen he would have done everything, including hard drugs. His lack of trust in his wife does not seem totally irrational, since she had only then told him that she was involved in fifteen relationships, all of them important. On the other hand, Michele is clearly still in love with her and feels a sense of failure because of their separation, or perhaps only anxiety when confronted with the idea of being alone. For the protagonist, autarchy proves to be an unachievable ideal, because he is unable to be autarchic in a positive sense: to be emotionally and sexually fulfilled when living alone. Michele is miserable while on his own, oscillating between melancholy, hysteria and aggression (usually directed towards his estranged wife), and often on the verge of an emotional breakdown. Michele is driven to look for an alternative both to traditional family life and to loneliness. He finds it temporarily (and perhaps unsatisfactorily) in a sort of informal commune, which he sets up with his friends who participate in the experimental theatre production. It starts when Michele agrees to the request of his friend Fabio, the director, to use his apartment to assemble the actors and prepare for the show. The director, in fact, spends progressively more and more time in Michele's apartment, sharing meals with him. Later, another member of the group, who had been talking all the time of finally leaving home, moves in with his luggage claiming that he has been thrown out by his parents. Furthermore, Michele joins the camp which Fabio organises for the actors. Here, however, he discovers that the structured camp life is not for him, as is suggested by his lonely excursions into the countryside, when he gazes at the sea, and eventually by his attempt to run away from the camp. His escape, however, is unsuccessful; he is captured by other members and forcefully returned to his tent.

The informal commune which is set up in Michele's house is close to what Gaeton Fonzi describes as a 'crash pad', although it also has some of the characteristics of an 'intentional community'.

Crash pads are generally populated by hippie types or teenie boppers on a runaway gig. It's usually a rented apartment financed by someone with a job or generous parents. Friends and strangers 'crash' the pad, come and go, stay as long as they like, may or may not kick in to help with expenses or maintenance. Everyone does what he wants and there is little group decision-making. A crash pad is just a place to stay, but some of them do take on the sense of a commune because, in addition to the common dwelling they inhabit (often without any semblance of privacy) the residents do share things and do establish group relationships, sometimes to the point where most of them derive a sense of security from the group. (Fonzi 1972: 182)

Intention, on the other hand, is by definition a principal characteristic of 'intentional communities'.

The members of this type of cooperative are attempting to establish in miniature a social system that will allow them to live as they think men should live ... The motivation for a 'prophetic' or 'utopian' community is more than economic or practical. It is to be faithful to a principle, to live according to a lifestyle that one believes in, to revolutionalise oneself *and* to provide an example for a revolutionary society. (Fonzi 1972: 183)

Fonzi also mentions 'cooperatives', which are practical, organised living arrangements, whose residents share the expenses of the dwelling and its upkeep, and sometimes subsistence (1972: 182).

As members of a model 'crash pad', Michele and his companions have no proper jobs, nor do they seek any. The flat that they inhabit, or where they spend long hours, is paid for by Michele's father (Michele once contacts him requesting the 'usual cheque', apparently to prevent viewers from wondering how he maintains himself). Nor is there any structure to their living, they come and go whenever they want to. They have no clear purpose for staying together – or, rather, their communal life is meant to fulfil a number of functions: to build a team of devoted and capable performers in the experimental play, to discuss and criticise the world in which they live, and simply to be together and share experiences. It is also not impossible that Michele uses his friends to help him bring up his child. Like the members of intentional communities, Michele and his friends rebel against mainstream society (of which a traditional, nuclear family was always a buttress and emblem), and dream about a revolution. Yet, they also appear rather unfocused and uncertain about their goals, never mentioning any means of achieving them.

Michele once claims to be bothered by a friend who always criticises him because he never lived in a commune; his comments suggest that he does feel guilty about this, and that he never found the courage to do it. When, towards the end of the narrative, he discovers that Fabio was a member of a commune all along, he is surprised, perhaps a little envious of his friend, and is even more shocked when he finds out that the commune is Buddhist – 'Italian Buddhists?' he asks, partly ironic and partly admiring. Judging by Michele's attempted escape from the training camp, he favours an informal 'crash pad', rather than more structured communal arrangements. Perhaps, the 'crash pad' does not involve the type of commitment and therefore the courage that joining a commune requires. As Moss Kanter has observed, informality, the lack of structure, clearly defined goals and leadership are the typical characteristics of short-lived communities: 'The prospects for most of today's anarchistic communes are dim; they lack the commitment-building practices of the successful communities of the nineteenth century' (Kanter 1972: 178). As if to confirm this view, Moretti suggests that the commune represented in *Io sono un autarchico* has little chance of surviving. At the end of the film, everyone goes his or her own way, and Michele remains on his own; even his son, as was previously mentioned, is returned to his mother. The film ends on a sombre note. A lonely Michele is not at all autarchic, instead he gives the impression of a man who is deeply unhappy and whose most important needs are by no means met.

Ecce Bombo also deals with the issue of communal living, as opposed to living in a traditional family. Here, however, we witness a more radical alternative arrangement to the nuclear family; furthermore, the family from which the protagonist seeks refuge is different from that in the earlier film, and it conforms to the Italian norm, with both parents and their two children living together in one household. The son and protagonist, Michele, is a university student; the daughter, Valentina, is in secondary school. We assume that the father is the breadwinner, as the mother is a housewife. Michele's position of son in the family structure allows him to keep a certain distance from the other members, something that would be far more difficult for a husband and a father, as was the case in *Io sono un autarchico*. Although superficially the family functions well, as suggested by the habit of regularly sharing meals and discussing family matters together, it also displays several symptoms of being dysfunctional and in crisis. The father (in common with the father in *La messa è finita*) is largely detached from the other members of the family, and is immersed in a life of newspapers, books and television. In one episode we even see him cover his entire body with a blanket when sitting in an armchair, as if to avoid seeing what is around him and to become invisible to the rest of the family. Not surprisingly, this solipsistic 'head of the family' knows little about his daughter's participation in the school strike and his son's interests. Neither does he understand the feelings of his wife, who comes across as the most frustrated person in the household. She cooks, cleans, serves her husband and children, and is expected to take care of everybody, yet her devotion is barely appreciated. Nobody, perhaps with the exception of Valentina, listens to her opinions or treats her with respect, and she takes all the blame when something goes wrong. The mother also appears to be sexually frustrated – in bed there is always a physical distance between her and her husband, who pays no attention to her (he even sings on one occasion). Moreover, unlike her husband who goes to work and when at home disappears in front of the television set or at his desk, the mother has no refuge, has no space of her own, and is ever exposed to the eyes of those with whom she lives. The level of her loneliness and unhappiness comes across in the episode in which we see her drinking alcohol on her own, sitting at the kitchen table. At the same time, one gets the impression that it is mainly thanks to her that the Apicellas continue to be a family, as she acts as mediator between the members. Without her, they would be totally fragmented.

Michele is critical of both his mother and his sister. He sadistically reproaches the former for her manner of speaking, for expressing opinions that he considers unintelligent, and for the way in which she brings up his sister. On one occasion he even says that he would like to be the only person at home to take responsibility for Valentina. Michele defends Valentina and her choices in the face of their parents, but he does so only in order to subvert their authority, and exercise his own instead. In fact, he criticises his sister for her table manners, disapproves of her taking part in the occupation of her school, and objects when she has sex with her boyfriend. At the same time, he sleeps with a stream of women, including the wife of one of his friends. In this way, he comes across as one who believes that there should be two sexual mores: one for men, one for women. This attitude is considered typical of Italian (or perhaps Mediterranean) men, who tend to be despotic and overprotective with their mothers and sisters, and to consider them as different from other women: whereas women outside the house are seen by them as prey for their sexual desires, mothers and sisters are treated as saintly figures who should be protected from other males. Such an attitude to women conforms to Freud's opinion that men 'split women symbolically and erotically into ... mothers and sisters, on the one hand, and prostitutes on the other. The former cannot be sexually desired, though they are supposed to be the kind of woman a man should marry; the latter, though they are maritally and socially forbidden, can be sexually desired' (Chodorow 1991: 22).

Even more than he points to the imperfections of the women in his family, Michele is aware and critical of the shortcomings of his father. He rarely talks to him, as if holding him in contempt, and when he does he usually criticises him and accuses him of behaving like a victim. At times he tries to annoy him, and to attract his attention, as when he empties the contents of the rubbish bin onto his desk. The resentment towards his father is also conveyed by an imaginary scene, set in a wood, in which the father tries to catch small Michele with a lasso. The only moment when these two men are together and communicate with each other, albeit in a limited way, is when they watch a light entertainment show on television.

The father-son relationship, as presented by Moretti, bears strong associations with that described by Robert Bly in his book *Iron John*, published for the first time in 1990, but referring to processes that took place long before that date, reaching even as far back as the industrial revolution. In opposition to Freud and Jung, who stressed the figure of the mother in the bringing up of children of both sexes, Bly insists on the centrality of the father in the development of the male child. The author argues that contemporary men have lost their power and feel emasculated, even redundant. The causes that he indicates include the process of industrialisation, which provoked the split between the traditional connection between home and work, a split that prevented the sons from seeing their fathers at work and thus from taking them as role models; a proliferation of negative images of men in the media; and the women's movement, although Bly reluctantly acknowledges the impact of the last factor. One of the most important consequences, according to Bly, is the lessening of the fathers' authority: 'When a father sits down at the table, he seems weak and insignificant, and we all sense that fathers no longer fill as large a space in the room as nineteenth-century fathers did' (Bly 1990: 98). The 'diminishing of fathers' has far-reaching implications for the sons:

In our time, when the father shows up as an object of ridicule (as he does ... on television), or a fit field for suspicion (as he does in *Star Wars*), or a bad tempered fool (when he comes home from the office with no teaching), or a weak puddle of indecision (as he stops inheriting kingly radiance), the son has a problem. How does he imagine his own life as a man? (Bly 1990: 99)

Barbara Ehrenreich refers to similar problems in her essay 'The Decline of Patriarchy' (1995), and corroborates her thesis by the increase in the proportion of households that are 'female headed', a declining interest on the part of men in supporting women as wives and full-time homemakers, as well as in having children themselves. Ehrenreich also suggests that contemporary men no longer depend on women for physical survival; neither do they need women to express their social status. Ehrenreich does not go as far back as the beginning of industrialisation to discover the roots of this phenomenon, but she puts forward the decline of male wages, which is a phenomenon of the post-World War Two era, as a crucial factor in the current status quo. Although both Bly and Ehrenreich base their research on American men and their families, many of their observations can be applied to European countries, including Italy. According to Ginsborg, the lack of a male role model constituted a major problem for young Italian men in the 1980s and 1990s, and we will suggest that this problem started earlier than the 1980s, even as far back as the end of World War Two. The most important causes of the 'diminishing of fathers' in post-war Italian society are: first, the disastrous end of Fascism, an ideology that had based its success on men seen as virile soldiers, workers, husbands and fathers, and that had promoted the idea that Italy and its men were invincible; second, the process of rapid industrialisation of the country that brought the men to the factories, encouraged urbanisation and emigration and broke the traditional link between man and earth (as well as man and house); third, the process of modernisation of the country, with the consequent challenges to long-established values, and the emancipation of women and of the younger generations. The fact that the 'diminishing of fathers' is a recurrent theme in post-war Italian cinema testifies to the importance of this process in Italian society. Some key Italian films that deal with this theme include Vittorio De Sica's *Ladri di biciclette* (*Bicycle Thieves*, 1948), with a father whose authority vacillates throughout the narrative only to be crushed at the end, and who was humiliated by two years of unemployment during which his young son was the breadwinner for the family; Luchino Visconti's *Rocco e i suoi fratelli* (*Rocco and His Brothers*, 1960), in which the crisis of traditional values suffered by a family from the South when it relocates to Milan is accentuated by the absence of the paternal figure, who had recently died; Marco Bellocchio's *I pugni in tasca* (*Fists in the Pocket*, 1965), the devastating portrait of a sick bourgeois family in which the father is once again absent, and the mother blind; and the Taviani brothers' *Padre padrone* (1977), a film in which Moretti himself played a small role, and which tells of an authoritarian and brutal Sardinian father eventually defeated by the son's will to study and progress.

Bly enumerates a number of ways in which sons react to the metaphorical disappearance of their fathers. In practice, he tacitly advises young men to look for comfort and strength in each other, distancing themselves from women. Bly's book had an influence on all-male discussion groups and male therapy sessions. As if anticipating the findings of Bly (which are not short on controversy), and his recipe to counteract the perilous state in which young, metaphorically fatherless men found themselves, Michele, together with his friends, sets up an all-male support group. His disillusionment with his father cannot be regarded as the only reason why he seeks intellectual and emotional fulfilment outside his family, but there is no doubt that the inadequacy of his father plays a part in his search for a surrogate family. The male friends do not form a proper commune, as they still live in their own houses, but in some ways seem to have more in common than the group of friends depicted in *Io sono un autarchico*. They model themselves on feminist organisations, which became widespread in the 1970s, meet regularly to talk about political issues as well as their personal problems, and organise excursions. It can be argued that together they create a distinctive style, marked by a critical attitude to everything that surrounds them, self-mockery and an affinity for surrealism. Accordingly, they come across as somewhat blasé and immature. Their political slant is obviously left-wing, since the very fact of setting up a male commune as an alternative to a nuclear family was typically an oppositional, left-wing practice. In a large part of Marxist discourse, in fact, the family had negative connotations, being associated with the exploitation of women, a 'bourgeois mental framework', and putting personal interest above the welfare of the society as a whole (see Bronfenbrenner 1972). Engels emphasised the enslavement embodied in the family by noting that the word 'familia' originally referred to the total number of slaves belonging to one man (Engels 1972: 121). The group in *Ecce Bombo*, in truth, lacks a clear political project, and we often have the suspicion that they stay together on the basis of a shared goliardic spirit, as well as for a more or less subconscious desire to postpone their entrance into adulthood. For instance, a comparison with the women's groups on which they model themselves shows that, in contrast with such organisations, in which sexual difference was regarded as a crucial issue, the male self-support group in Moretti's film is remarkably uninterested in gender politics. In most cases we may imagine women taking part in their discussions and activities without their character changing. Indeed, Olga, the schizophrenic friend of Mirko, one of the members of the group, often comes into the room when the friends are having discussions and they accept, if not welcome, her presence. They are by no means enemies of women, as testified by the care Mirko takes of Olga, by the fact that one of them, Cesare, is married, and by Michele's restless pursuit of female partners. The only time when their behaviour may be accused of sexism is when they jokingly dedicate over the telephone an aria from *Tosca* to an attractive girl whom they previously met. On this occasion, their behaviour is condemned by Olga, who claims that their repeated phone calls could annoy or offend the girl. However, the joke is rather a sign of their 'laddish' interest in women, their playfulness and their immature relationship with the other sex. Nevertheless, it can be suggested that feminism had an impact on their self-perception and attitude to women. In particular, they do not take their gender identity for granted and regard it as something natural, as presumably their fathers did. On the contrary, they discuss and search for it. They also pay attention to their appearance, and are willing to treat women as their equals. There is a certain vulnerability about them, which was unknown or at least unacceptable in the previous generation of Italian men, as shown in a scene in which Cesare, who is the only married member of the group, weeps in the bathroom because his wife betrayed him and he is worried that she will leave him forever. Their willingness to question their masculinity finds confirmation in the following declaration by Moretti: 'In *Ecce Bombo* there is the parody of a previous experience of mine in a male "self-awareness" group. It was the only time when I was in the vanguard in my life, also because in 1974 that was a novelty which was looked on with suspicion by the most serious and self-confident militants' (Moretti quoted in Giovannini, Magrelli & Sesti 1986:

32). In other words, 'serious and self-confident militants' were generally afraid to examine their own maleness.

The informal character of the 'male brotherhood' gives the group a creative edge (on one occasion the members, inspired by the atmosphere of their meeting, appear to produce poetry, albeit with poor results), and allows the members to stay in close contact with other social institutions, such as their own families, to form relations with other people, and to pursue their own, idiosyncratic interests. Yet, the lack of a well defined common goal and strategy, as well as of a specific code of behaviour, poses a serious threat to the cohesion and sustainability of the male circle, somewhat like in *Io sono un autarchico*. Consequently, one of the members eventually decides to join a different organisation, which is a formal, Stalinist-style commune, and in the end the circle is practically disbanded or, more precisely, abandoned, with each member literally heading his own way. This is shown in the last scene of the film in which the friends, and many other acquaintances, set off on a trip to see Olga, but only Michele (who was initially very reluctant) actually visits her – the rest find other distractions on the way and never reach their destination. The film closes on Michele and Olga looking at each other. It is significant that Michele in the end faces Olga and looks into her eyes; as a critic has rightly noticed, Michele's histrionic exhibitionism and his attempt to channel the schizophrenic suffering are the prelude of the condition of the protagonist of the next film, *Sogni d'oro* (cf. De Bernardinis 2001: 51). In fact, some scenes in *Ecce Bombo* gain additional significance in the context of Michele's future incarnations in *Sogni d'oro* and then in *Bianca*. Take, for example, the episode in which a group of Valentina's friends gather in her room to discuss the occupation of the school. Michele neither joins in, nor ignores the group, but observes them from his hiding place behind a door. We also see that he himself is being observed by his father standing in the corridor. On the whole, it feels as if the men in the Apicella household prefer to be (passive) voyeurs than (active) participants – an attitude which will be shared by the protagonists of both *Sogni d'oro* and *Bianca*. Michele's constant censuring and reproaching of both his sister and his mother, his occasional violence towards members of his family, and his habit of sleeping with many women without being committed to any of them also give us a foretaste of the older Michele – who will be very critical of other people and their families and who will look for an ideal household, without being able to conform to the high standards that he imposes on others.

Yet, on the whole, Michele in *Ecce Bombo*, in common with the protagonist of *Io sono un autarchico*, is a man with a healthy personality, even if not one that can be described as particularly easygoing. It is when his ties with his old friends are lost, as shown in the subsequent 'Apicella films', that his mental health deteriorates and he becomes deeply unhappy. Hence, it could be argued that *Io sono un autarchico* and *Ecce Bombo* are subtle eulogies of 'surrogate families', particularly for men who are unable to fulfil the obligations of family life, while still needing human contact and close relationships.

The search for a perfect family

In the films from *Sogni d'oro* to *Palombella rossa* Moretti constructs Michele Apicella as a character who desperately needs close human contact, while at the same time being at odds with his own family and social milieu. Many characteristics of the previous versions of Michele are still present in these films, including one that we have not yet discussed: his narcissism. Michele's inability in *Io sono un autarchico* and in *Ecce Bombo* to accept people for what they are, his autoerotism, and his way of considering himself to be at the centre of the universe, are all signs of his infantile narcissism. In subsequent films, and particularly in *Sogni d'oro* and in *Bianca*, it becomes evident that his narcissism prevents Michele from having normal relationships with women, and from forming his own family. As Mariella Cruciani suggested:

> That which prevents Michele Apicella from fulfilling his desire of normality is a pathological fixation to his ideal Ego, which, conceived as a narcissistic ideal of omnipotence, does not limit itself to the union of Ego and Id, but involves a primary identification with another being who is endowed with omnipotence: the mother. (Cruciani 2000: 74)

The protagonist in *Sogni d'oro*, who is a successful film director in his early thirties, has two important relationships in his life. One is with his mother, with whom he lives, the other with an attractive young woman named Silvia – but this relationship belongs to the world of dream rather than to reality. Michele's mother is a retired teacher and, although she is not an intellectual, neither is she ignorant or stupid. In spite of that, Michele treats her badly, incessantly criticising her cooking and ridiculing her political views, which he rejects as being too stereotypical and commonplace for his sophisticated political taste. The climax of his dissatisfaction is a scene in which, during a dinner with his mother and his assistants Nicola and Claudio, Michele first sings some revelatory lines that clearly refer to his mother ('No, don't believe her, for her you're only a toy, the whim of a moment, but for me you are life itself'), then he beats her up, after which the mother insists that he moves out of her house. Michele, however, refuses exclaiming: 'I do not want to overcome my Oedipus!'

The reference to Freud has added meaning, as the young director is making a film entitled *Freud's Mother*, about an old madman who thinks that he is Freud. He still lives with his mother and cannot detach himself from her. Similarly, Michele's situation mirrors that of a failed Oedipus – as if the protagonist had not overcome the unconscious set of loving and hostile drives that the child, in a particular phase of his psychological and sexual growth, experiences in relation to his parents, and especially the longing for his mother and consequent rivalry with the father. A successful Oedipus for the male child entails that he give up his identification with and his love for the mother, and identify with the father, thus entering adulthood and becoming able to develop relationships with other women. The oedipal phase is particularly difficult as the child, according to Freud, lives in fear that his father will punish him for his desire, and castrate him. In *Sogni d'oro* there are further references to the complex love/hate relationship with the mother that is experienced in childhood. Michele, for instance, finds it very difficult to shoot a particular scene of his film, that of the 'Fort/Da', of the child who plays with a reel of thread, making it disappear and then reappear – according to Freud, this game represents the fear of the child of being left by the mother, and his need to exercise a control over her comings and goings.

The reason for which Michele did not successfully complete his oedipal phase is most probably the absence of the father. As Cruciani reminds us, 'In the process of individualisation, of separation from the mother, the paternal figure is fundamental because, with its presence, it does not leave the child in the midst of his castration anxiety, but offers him an alliance and a direction' (Cruciani 2000: 75). In this sense, Bly and Freud do agree on the importance of the paternal figure in the development of the boy. In *Sogni d'oro*, the father is completely absent; in the other Apicella films the paternal figure is seen as weak and ineffectual. Michele as a father in *Io sono un autarchico* is not a strong figure; as Cruciani suggests, the father/son relationship in this film is reversed, and Michele gives the impression that he considers his child to be a rival, as if he would like to be the child in his place (Cruciani 2000: 77). By painting fathers as weak, childlike figures, who make mistakes, demand understanding and ask for help, rather than as strong role models for their children, Moretti seems to agree with Bly's reading of the 'diminishing of fathers' in our society. Interestingly, fathers in the Apicella films are never seen working, and are often retired men who feel at a loss in the home, again confirming that – as in Bly's theory – work has a fundamental role in the construction of masculinity.

Not only is the father absent in *Sogni d'oro*; unlike in *Io sono un autarchico* and in *Ecce Bombo* there are no male support groups to help Michele make the transition from childhood to adulthood, or at least to provide an alternative space for activity and relationships. On the whole, Michele's love for and attachment to his mother confines him to his childhood home. Moretti emphasises this by representing his character as disproportionately attached to mementoes of his youth and to boyish games. Take, for example, the scene in which Michele finds a miniature football game in his room and plays with it compulsively. This game, as opposed to normal football requiring a number of players, also conveys Michele's solipsism. Another sign of his solipsism is the large blanket that he uses to cover himself, as if he needed extra warmth and protection from the outside world. Michele's father in *Ecce Bombo* also used a blanket to cover himself completely – accordingly, it may be that Italian men do learn something from their fathers, but these are negative lessons of solitude and withdrawal.

Michele's attitude towards his mother should be placed in the context of the mother/son relationship in contemporary Italy. As Laura Laurenzi observes, commenting on some statistics concerning the frequency of contacts between Italian mothers and their adult sons: 'Italian men – whether single, married, co-habiting, separated or divorced – demonstrate an evident reluctance, whether from choice or necessity, to distance themselves from the maternal embrace and from that formidable supplier of services constituted by a matriarchal home in which everything functions' (quoted in Ginsborg 2001: 79). At the same time, as Paul Ginsborg observes, Italian sons do not simply seek their mothers' company (although it is an important factor in their closeness), but expect them 'to be little short of saints' (ibid.). Consequently, the mother's unwillingness or inability to fulfil the high standard of maternal care required of her by her son is a source of frustration to the son and, in extreme cases, as demonstrated by Moretti, ends with his revenge or punishment of the 'underperforming mother'.

Michele's attachment to his mother and to his childhood world renders him impotent in relationships with other women, his potential lovers and wives. Nowhere is this more evident than in his attitude to Silvia. Whenever she turns up, Michele is nearby, but instead of trying to make contact and seduce her, he predominantly limits himself to spying on her. Eventually, when she does show an interest in him, he runs away from her. Michele's behaviour is paradoxical – the more he desires something, the more he is afraid of failing, and the less able he is to conquer the object of his desire. His actions are marked by both sadism and masochism; sadism, because he hurts the people he loves, masochism, because he also hurts himself, dooming himself to solitude, erotic and emotional frustration, and passivity. The fact that Silvia appears only in Michele's dreams and in scenes whose ontological status is ambivalent, such as in the last episode during which Michele is transformed into a werewolf, strengthens our point that in this film Michele is unable to leave his past behind and start a life of his own, and rather dangerously retreats into a fantasy world.

Michele's brutal treatment of his mother as a punishment for her supposed inadequacy, as well as his fantasising about Silvia, also demonstrate that he

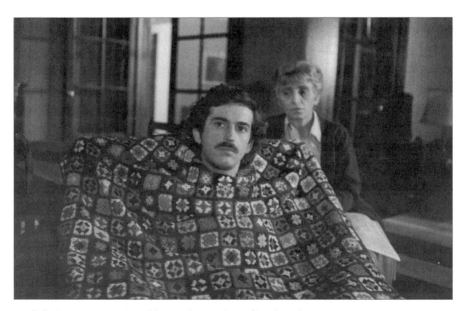

Michele (Nanni Moretti) and his mother in *Sogni d'oro* (1981)

is unable to accept other people for what they are, and to bridge the gap between the ideal and reality. The fact that, as an object of his erotic dreams, he chooses a beautiful and mysterious woman (who is more attractive than Michele's female partners in *Io sono un autarchico* and *Ecce Bombo*) adds to the impression that he has very high standards in relation to women. The climax of Michele's withdrawal from social life is his transformation into a werewolf at the end of the film. As is the case with many scenes in *Sogni d'oro*, we are uncertain whether Michele really changes into a werewolf, or if it is simply another dream. This, however, hardly influences the viewer's diagnosis of Michele – he is a madman, a person with two irreconcilable lives and identities, a schizophrenic.

In *Bianca*, Moretti further develops the themes of male desire and frustration, and of schizophrenia, a condition that we have already addressed in the first chapter, and that we will discuss in greater depth below. This time the protagonist is a newly qualified teacher of mathematics starting his first job at a secondary school in Rome. He moves into a flat with a large balcony, from which he is able to observe his neighbours. He makes the acquaintance of Siro Siri, an elderly man who lives one floor above him, and who tries to become his friend, as well as of a young, unmarried couple living in the flat next to his, Massimiliano and Aurora, who instead do not warm to him. To facilitate his relationship with the couple, Michele even orders a hand-knitted jumper from Aurora, who earns her living in this way.

Michele seems to be motivated by two desires, one of which is to find a girlfriend. Siro Siri, who is a womaniser, encourages him in this pursuit, even more than Michele would like: he invites him to meet his young female friends, and one day takes him to a park with a large pond, where people boat. Here, he convinces Michele to rent a boat and sit in it, in the middle of the pond, dressed in white and reading Proust. Siro believes that a woman, admiring Michele's intellectual aura and fin-de-siècle elegance, will eventually approach him, something that does not happen. Michele believes that everybody around him is in a romantic relationship, except for him. His sexual frustration becomes evident in the surreal scene at the beach when, induced by the pervasive eroticism of a number of couples kissing under the sun, he lays on one of the few single women who are sunbathing, thus provoking the enraged and disgusted reaction of the other people. Eventually, however, Michele finds the woman of his dreams: Bianca, the new French teacher in his school. Her mysterious, almost supernatural apparition suggests that she may even be the materialisation of Michele's dreams. Although initially she remains aloof from Michele because she already has a partner, she soon succumbs to his charms and, at a certain stage, even appears to be more interested in their being together than does Michele.

The second desire which occupies Michele's mind is that there be love and harmony in couples and in families. Michele wants to see only happy relationships around him, and is deeply disturbed when couples whom he assumed were fulfilling his ideal fail to do so. Moreover, he is prepared to intervene in order to 'save' them. We witness several cases of such expectations, disappointments and interventions during the course of the film. When he finds out that Aurora betrays Massimiliano, for instance, Michele is deeply upset; shortly afterwards the couple are found dead, and at the end of the narrative we discover that Michele murdered them as a punishment for the disappointment that they caused him. Michele is also deeply involved in the lives of another couple, who are long-time friends of his. Their relationship too is in crisis, and each of them has found a new partner. Michele, however, tries to convince them to stay together, pestering them with telephone calls and visits. In the end he kills them, together with their new partners.

Michele also becomes involved in the romantic life of Bianca, visiting the flat where she lives with her boyfriend. Contrary to what we might expect, he does not look for signs of problems between Bianca and her partner that might improve his chances of winning her over from his rival, but rather seeks evidence of harmony in their relationship. Similarly, he seems to be blissfully happy and deeply moved to observe Bianca and her boyfriend holding hands and talking in the middle of the street, even if in reality the meeting marks their separation. This episode demonstrates that for Michele it is more important that a couple be perfect than that he be happy himself. Furthermore, if we consider Michele's misgivings about living with Bianca, and ultimately his rejection of her love, this episode suggests that he prefers to be an observer and to act on behalf of other people, for their (wrongly defined) happiness, rather than for himself.

One possible explanation for Michele's behaviour is his fear of failure: having failed to find a perfect couple, he dreads that his own attempts to be involved in a good relationship are likewise doomed. This fear can be read as a crisis of traditional macho masculinity as, according to the stereotype, a true man is never afraid of relationships, and always takes an active role in them. Michele's fear, though, is pathological, and is better read as fear of being abandoned, primarily by the mother (who in Freudian terms is the paradigm for a man's relationships with women), secondarily by his partner, as testified by the words with which Michele rejects Bianca: 'Anyway, sooner or later you would leave me … I must defend myself.' This fear paralyses Michele and urges him to escape, in order to avoid risk. In psychoanalytic terms, Mariella Cruciani (2000) reads Michele's strategy of defence from pain as a 'limitation of the Ego', which is not a pathological state, but a normal stage of the Ego's development. Referring to Anna Freud, Cruciani shows how Michele's particularly strong Super-Ego induces him to avoid the satisfaction of his desires, without however preventing him from taking an interest in other people's romantic and sexual lives. In other words, Michele lives the lives of others in order to avoid living his own life, and when he pushes Bianca away and then kills his friends, he gives up any form of gratification.

This reading gains credence if we look at the Apicella saga as a whole, in which the various films represent stages in Michele's development. On the other hand, if we only focus on *Bianca*, we are forced to observe that Michele's is, in this case, more than a moment of faltering masculinity or a normal phase of development: it is a crisis that leads to a mental illness, of which Michele's murders are the ultimate testimony. Michele's behaviour and his fate (he ends up in jail), corroborate the argument that, in contemporary times, as Roger Horrocks puts it, 'patriarchal masculinity cripples men' (Horrocks 1994: 25).

In an interview with Jean A. Gili, Moretti explains the absence of Michele's family from *Bianca* by saying that he did not want to offer a simple psychological explanation for his protagonist's behaviour. Regardless of Michele's childhood history, which is not disclosed to us, Moretti suggests that in this film Michele has an extremely idealised vision of the family (Gili 1987: 17). The gap between his real and imaginary childhood results in him being metaphorically trapped in the past, as indicated by a large picture of Michele when he was a small boy that dominates his sitting room, as well as by his affinity for sport and childhood games (whenever he sees a ball he cannot resist kicking it), and by his love for sweets. Michele is not only divided between past and present, but also between his daytime life as a law-abiding citizen and teacher, and his nocturnal murderous activity. The parallels with the double life of Doctor Jekyll and Mister Hyde suggest that, like Doctor Jekyll, Michele may have no power over that part of himself who attacks and murders innocent people.

A double life and lack of intentionality, withdrawal from social life and impotence, absolute predominance of the inner life, combined with an experience of almost god-like power over the lives of fellow human beings, and solipsistic grandiosity, are features which characterise Michele in *Sogni d'oro* and *Bianca*, and which are also typical of schizophrenia. The two character's schizophrenic condition is conveyed by Moretti not only through the narrative, but also visually. Many, if not the majority, of the scenes in *Sogni d'oro* represent Michele's dreams and fantasies. Even the episodes that are set in real time and space have a very subjective character. A surreal, subjective quality also characterises much of *Bianca*, in particular the scenes on the beach and in the park, as well as many episodes set in the school. Again, as in *Sogni d'oro*, we are given the impression of seeing the world through Michele's eyes, and his perceptions are far from normal. Moreover, he often acts in a way which suggests his feeling of omnipotence or, on the contrary, his complete inability to control himself, his being at the mercy of dark forces. Again, such experiences are typical of schizophrenia. As Louis A. Sass observes:

> Schizophrenics will often experience the world as having a derealised, subjectivised quality. This may coincide with a sense of almost divine importance or omnipotence, as if patients' awareness of their own subjectivity ensured their role as the transcendental centre or divine foundation of the universe … But the schizophrenic can also experience his or her own perceptions and thoughts as thinglike phenomena existing at a remove, as objects of observation or as subjects to external forces. (Sass 1997: 210)

The causes of schizophrenia are largely unknown. Some scholars attribute them to the physical constitution of a patient, such as neurobiological abnormalities, others blame the social and psychological circumstances of the schizophrenic, particularly his family situation (see Jackson 1960). The fact that there are profound similarities between modernity and schizophrenia as regards the nature of selfhood and self-experience, and taking into account the increased number of cases of schizophrenia in the modern industrialised West in comparison with other mental disorders suffered by Westerners, leads Sass to suggest that modernity (and late modernity, or postmodernity in particular) is very conducive to this disease. Sass quotes, amongst others, the sociologist Anthony Giddens, who 'stresses the dynamic, rapidly transforming quality of modern social institutions and practices, as well as a concomitant disembedding of these institutions and practices from their grounding in custom and tradition' (Sass 1997: 219). It is easy to imagine, according to Sass, 'how transformations such as these might foster schizophrenic forms of pathology – by encouraging social withdrawal and negativism, emotional flatness, intense self-consciousness … sense of inner division, and feelings of derealisation and ontological insecurity' (Sass 1997: 220).

At least in some cases, schizophrenia is not only a result of modern life, but also a symptom of rejection of modern life and of rebellion against it. Such a diagnosis perfectly suits Michele in *Bianca*. It appears as if he is caught in a temporal 'black hole': the world around him has changed immensely since he was a child, while he remained the same. His ideas about social life in general and family life in particular are rooted in the patriarchal Catholic tradition which by the 1980s had been largely rejected in Italy, or at least modified to take account of the new socio-economic situation. The gap between the new reality and Michele's set of values is revealed in his ideal vision of the family as a completely stable environment, where parents live for their children and children obey and respect their parents simply because they are parents, while real people around him have affairs, change partners, divorce, or have children outside marriage. The same gap is also revealed in Michele's discomfort at work. The school where he begins his career is ultra-liberal in a surreal way, as suggested by its name: the Marilyn Monroe School. Pictures of pop stars hang on the walls, there are slot machines in the staff room, and jukeboxes in the classrooms. Moreover, the school employs a psychotherapist to help teachers with their daily problems. In spite of his young age, Michele is less than impressed by the school's progressive ethos, and would probably favour a more conservative institution. On the other hand, rather than disagreeing with the teaching methods, Michele seems once again to be scared of failing (for example, he reacts angrily when a pupil challenges him in class, rather than admitting to gaps in his mathematical knowledge), and of being exposed (as when he refuses the help of the psychotherapist). At school, Michele gives vent to his frustration, as when he improvises a physical education lesson after observing Bianca talking to other people; one of the pupils refuses to submit to his drill, and Michele beats him up. Even students are the object of Michele's obsessive surveillance. For instance, he is unable to hide his outrage when he finds out that the family of a pupil who invited him to his home is not a 'proper' family, as the husband is 'only' a stepfather to his wife's children. Moretti shows sympathy for his troubled protagonist, but there is no doubt that he regards him as mentally ill and a social outsider. The message of the film is twofold. On the one hand, it suggests that people like Michele, of authoritarian, conservative views, must adjust to reality rather than attempt to force others to conform to their ideals. At the same time, Moretti ridicules the school where Michele works, and by extension, the ultra-liberal discourse which had become fashionable at the time he made his film, thus pointing to the malfunctions of society and to the new relaxed mores as being (at least partly) responsible for Michele's condition.

Perfect or 'normal' families are also of utmost interest to the main character in *La messa è finita*, a priest named Giulio. According to Moretti, 'It is possible that the protagonist of *La messa è finita* is named Michele as well. I think priests often change their name when they are ordained. This one is named Don Giulio – Don Michele didn't sound right – but perhaps before becoming a priest his name was Michele' (Gili 1987: 14). Taking into account this quotation and the strong link between this and the previous films, it makes sense to see *La messa è finita* as an Apicella film. Consequently, we will read the protagonist's unrest on two levels: as that of a priest when confronted with a secularised society, and as yet another stage in Michele Apicella's development. Confirming this view, in an interview Moretti said that '*La messa è finita* is not a film about priests' (Moretti quoted in Detassis 1986b: 48); in another interview, he explained that he made a film about a priest because he was interested in a character who, by definition, is expected to take care of other people, and that he was not at all interested in making a film about the crisis of faith in contemporary Italy, or about 'being a priest today' (Moretti quoted in De Bernardinis 1998: 7).

As a matter of fact, Don Giulio is an unusual priest; extreme intransigence, intolerance and even contempt often surface in his attitude towards others, bringing to mind the various embodiments of Michele Apicella, and in particular that in *Bianca*, in which the protagonist displayed a similar obsession with perfect families and couples, as well as a dislike of other people, as he once confessed to the school psychotherapist. Both men react in the same way to the gap between their ideal and reality: they become angry, neurotic and violent, feelings that render them impotent in their relationships with other people and unhappy with themselves. Although Giulio cannot be described as schizophrenic, he experiences a deep professional and personal crisis. As was the case for Michele in *Bianca*, Don Giulio's tragedy is that, despite everything, he still needs other people, and particularly his friends and family. Reading Giulio's character and behaviour in the light of the previous Apicella films, we suggest that Giulio is a man who cannot detach himself from his childhood, and who needs everybody to continue to be as they were, or as they seemed to be, when he was a boy. The fact that people have changed destroys the illusion of a happy, perfect childhood, an illusion to which Giulio is desperately attached.

On the other hand, Giulio is not just another Michele Apicella: in *La messa è finita* the Catholic background and traditionalism of the main character, which in *Bianca* was only hinted at, is openly enunciated and placed at the centre of the film's discourse. The very institution that Giulio represents is at odds with many of the 'inventions' of modern life, particularly divorce, contraception, the legalisation of abortion and the normalisation of extramarital sex. It seems that his views did not give rise to any difficulty when he worked as a priest in a rural parish, on the island of Ventotene; on the contrary, he was very popular there. The situation changes when he returns to Rome ten years later, to take over a small parish in the periphery. He soon discovers that he is out of tune with his parishioners, his friends, even his own family. He does not understand their problems; he is unable to identify with their choices. Emotionally and intellectually, he remains distant from them. The reasons underlying his lack of understanding and disapproval of others are dictated by the gap between his expectations of how people should live their lives and the new reality that surrounds him. Giulio assumes that the values and rules which he learnt when he was a child and which he preached as a priest in the rural parish are as relevant now as they were in the past. Yet the real world around him is very fluid. Values that were previously widely accepted and respected are now discarded. People no longer form a community, and everybody is solely preoccupied with his or her private world. Giulio finds it difficult to reach people, both emotionally and physically, as is the case with two of his old friends: Saverio, who after having been left by his partner lives locked up in his flat and does not want to see anybody, and Andrea, who is incarcerated for affiliation to a terrorist group, and who does not want to talk to his old friends either.

Due to his personal convictions even more than to his religious beliefs, Giulio tries to convince people to stay together, not to have abortions, not to quarrel nor to divorce. Yet perhaps because he never married and had children, he is unable to help anybody who experiences a family crisis. He simply does not have the practical sense and flexibility to identify with the problems of others, or even to gain their trust. Instead, he appears to judge every family against the unachievable ideal of the Holy Family. Despite his inflexibility, though, Giulio is not blind; his impotence upsets him, and he tries and searches for a way forward – for instance, he confesses to a monk that sometimes he feels so impotent that he feels like hitting people. Whereas Michele in *Bianca* allows his rigidity to turn into folly and becomes a murderer, Don Giulio resists this temptation and, towards the end, even seems to open up to a new, more flexible and reconciled attitude.

The discarding of Catholic values and lifestyles by contemporary Italians is particularly striking considering that Moretti's characters live near the Vatican, the heart of Roman Catholicism. The people whom Giulio approaches typically treat him with respect, even sympathy, but they remain unconvinced by his arguments. Consequently, he cannot influence their behaviour. There are no traditional or 'normal' families in sight. Paradoxically, the only family that approaches Giulio's ideal (and Michele's in *Bianca*) is the family of Antonio, the priest who worked in the parish some years before Giulio's arrival. The ex-priest loves his wife and his well-behaved son. However, as Catholic priests are not allowed to marry, he is also one of the greatest 'sinners' whom Giulio encounters. We learn that Antonio was forced to leave the parish and his profession, causing a scandal in the neighbourhood, and putting many local people off Catholicism. Initially, Giulio also condemns him, but after realising that his life is closer to the Christian ideal than that of most people whom he meets in Rome, he moderately warms to him. At one point, when he notices a tension between them, Giulio even tells the ex-priest and his wife that from them he expects marital harmony, not the conflicts which he observes everywhere else. On the other hand, this model family displeases Giulio, and one would say Moretti, for the way in which they educate their child: Antonio and his wife, in fact, often hint at their sexual life in front of the boy, and they pay excessive attention to him, as testified by the scene in which Giulio asks if it is the boy's birthday given all the presents that he has received, and his father replies that it is always his birthday. The discourse on single-child families will return in the episode 'Islands' in *Dear Diary*.

In *La messa è finita* Moretti also shows that the life of the Catholic clergy is lonely and alienating, as a result of which the priests are prone to the same unhappiness and misery that they are meant to alleviate in other people. Don Giulio seems conscious of this when he says to his sister, who has just separated from her partner and wants to abort his child, that 'true happiness is living with another person'. As Piera Detassis noticed, with this phrase he recognises that he has chosen solitude, and that happiness is elsewhere, thus that he will never be happy (Detassis 1986a: 46). To fight his solitude, Giulio, who inherited a flat near the church from his predecessors, moves back to his parents' apartment. In fact, he is uncomfortable in his flat, does not look after it and even avoids spending time there. By showing that even a Catholic priest (or maybe that Catholic priests in particular) cannot cope with solitude and need a real family, Moretti interrogates the Catholic rule of celibacy and perhaps the whole Catholic ethos of priesthood and family life. At the same time, he is far from approving of the reality that Giulio encounters back in Rome. The situation depicted in this film is similar to that in *Bianca*: it appears as if the old values and lifestyles, associated with patriarchy and the Catholic Church, are no longer suitable for contemporary Italy. Yet Moretti also shows that the values and lifestyles that replaced them only cause widespread loneliness and suffering. A large part of the sympathy directed by Moretti to his difficult, neurotic and internally divided protagonists results from the fact that both Michele in *Bianca* and Don Giulio in *La messa è finita* try to battle against this crisis, however incompetent, even harmful, their attempts are, whereas most people around them seem to accept living their lives in a moral vacuum.

Don Giulio's solitude is not only that of a priest who has chosen celibacy – it is also that of a male son who, having grown up, had to detach himself from his mother, but still cannot give up the memory and the thought of her safe and consoling presence in his life. It is mainly because of his mother that he prefers to stay with his family, rather than in his own flat, confirming the previously expressed view that Italian men are extremely reluctant to give up the maternal embrace, her comfort and her services. As was the case for the earlier Michele Apicella incarnations, Don Giulio's relationship with his mother is very strong; he is shocked and enraged when his father decides to leave her in order to move in with a much younger woman, and is devastated when his mother eventually commits suicide. As Mariella Cruciani noticed, the death of the mother is the event that 'makes the evolution of the protagonist necessary', because it cancels 'an important part of the son: the past, childhood as the only positive and real condition' (Cruciani 2000: 79). This is perhaps why, after the funeral of his mother, in the film's final scene Don Giulio smiles while watching his family, friends and parishioners sweetly dancing together in his church. Even if a dream-like sequence, it does lighten the film's atmosphere, as Moretti himself confirmed in an interview: Don Giulio's decision to leave the city and to go to Tierra del Fuego 'is simultaneously a victory and a defeat. I have the impression that at the end of the story Don Giulio accepts the choices of his sister, of his father (with more difficulty), of his friends who have chosen extreme and radical ways of behaving. Thus, he begins perhaps to understand that reality is more complicated than he imagined and wished' (Gili 1987: 17). On the other hand, Giulio's escape from the 'modern hell' of contemporary Rome, towards a faraway land almost devoid of human life, although suggesting that he will be able to preserve his sanity and carry on as a clergyman, also marks his defeat as a priest and as a man.

Surviving fatherhood

At the end of *Bianca* the main character declares that, 'It is sad to die without kids'. Talking of this film, Moretti once declared: 'Even if [*Bianca*] is, like my other films, strongly autobiographical, I am not Michele Apicella. I want to make films and have children, two ways of creating which, I believe, are not irreconcilable' (Moretti quoted in Masi 1984: 49). This attitude informs the narratives and ideology of the three most recent films by Moretti: *Dear Diary*, *Aprile* and *The Son's Room*. The importance that children and fatherhood acquired in Moretti's discourse on family (as well as in his life) is emphasised by a slight change in the logo of Moretti's company, Sacher Film – since *Aprile* Nanni rides his Vespa with a child clinging to his back.

The change of attitude in Moretti's protagonist starts, as we noticed, with *La messa è finita*, in which the death of his mother forces the character to 'grow up', to finally detach himself from childhood and embrace adulthood. Not surprisingly, in the subsequent film, *Palombella rossa*, Michele is the father of a teenage daughter, Valentina; the fact that neither his parents nor his wife are in sight conveys the impression that Michele is now able to confront his responsibilities on his own. The film mainly concentrates on Michele's political crisis, which reflects the wider crisis of Italian and world Communism in the 1980s, but the discourse on family is also present, although less central to the film's narrative and meaning. Michele's relationship with Valentina does not appear to be traditional, as seen when the father distracts the girl from her study in order to play with her. Nevertheless, whereas in *Io sono un autarchico* Michele appeared to be more childish than his child, we suggest that in *Palombella rossa* this is not the case, and that Moretti begins to sketch a form of fatherhood based on complicity and playfulness, and on the recognition of one's limits, rather than on the more traditional, authoritarian patriarchal approach which he had criticised in the senior Apicellas of the previous films. This 'new' paternal figure will emerge strongly in *Aprile*, and will also be found in *The Son's Room*.

As for *Dear Diary*, the discourse on family is prominent only in the fragment about Nanni's and his friend Gerardo's trip to the island of Salina, which is represented as a place inhabited by one-child families. As was previously mentioned, this type of family became the norm in Italy in the 1990s; consequently, the situation portrayed in the Salina episode can be regarded as metaphorical of that in the whole of Italy. By the use of caricature and grotesque, Moretti presents in a concise way typical causes and consequences of the Italian phenomenon of *il bambino negato* (the denied child). He includes a family who claim that they would love to have another child, but that their son, who is now a teenager, does not want any siblings. Another family does not explain why they did not have a second child, but their attitude to their son sheds light on their asceticism in this area: as they confess, in order to assure their boy's security and happiness they never left him with a babysitter. The reasons for such an extreme protective attitude are explained by Moretti in an interview:

Men and women [of my generation] for many years have resisted the idea of having children, they have even theorised about not wanting children. For our parents, it was normal to have children, one, two, three, four children … the opposite of my generation. Thus these parents often have only one child, and adopt a very protective attitude towards him or her. (Gili 1994: 13)

In his film, Moretti suggests that the scarcity of children in Salina produces a specific culture, one in which the child is the object of hyper-attention and hyper-affection and acquires significant power over his or her parents and their relationship with the outside world. This is encapsulated in the surreal scene in which Nanni tries to make a phone call, but cannot because the phone is always intercepted and answered by a child who, instead of passing the receiver directly to the parent, demands various services from the speaker, such as telling a story or making animal-like noises. As a result, Salina appears to be completely, albeit subtly, dominated and paralysed by children, who on the one hand are more intelligent and sophisticated than their peers in other cultures, and on the other force the adults to behave as if they were children themselves. Moretti's representation of the Salinans confirms the opinion formulated by the sociologists Padiglione and Pontalti that the overall result of the low fertility rate in Italy was 'to block the generations in a sort of reciprocal protection [*accudimento*] which was substantially infantilising' (quoted in Ginsborg 2001: 80). Yet, the author's attitude to the 'Salina family' and, by the same token, to the typical modern Italian family, is ambivalent. As Moretti has confirmed, 'This sequence has been filmed with affection, both for the children and for the parents' (Gili 1994: 13). Criticism of overprotective parents and overprotected children is, in fact, combined with a fascination and admiration for the inter-generational dialogue and family harmony observed there. The child functions like perfect 'glue' between his or her parents. This happiness and serenity are particularly remarkable in comparison with the dysfunctional families and relationships represented in Moretti's earlier films. Moreover, against the background of other Eolian islands, which are either stuck in the past or desperately trying to be progressive, Salina appears relatively genuine and at ease with itself.

In *Aprile* Moretti reveals a similar ambivalence towards the rearing of children 'Italian-style'. In many ways Silvia, Nanni and Pietro form a typical 1990s Italian family, which is not very different from those encountered by Nanni and his friend in Salina. Both parents are relatively mature: Moretti was over forty years old when Pietro was born, and his partner was probably over thirty. Both also have careers of their own: Nanni is a film director, Silvia works as a translator. It is suggested that the child was planned and both parents tried to prepare for his arrival as well as they could, following the advice of an obstetrician, learning about the various stages of the birth, decorating the nursery – and spending long hours deciding on the baby's name. Moreover, the child plays an important role in the lives of the extended families of Nanni and Silvia even before he is born. This is excellently portrayed in the humorous scene in which the two prospective grandmothers show Silvia the clothes which they bought or handmade for their future grandson. The number of these clothes, especially of the pairs of miniature shoes made by Nanni's mother, seems excessive and Nanni becomes very excited and impatient to show them to Silvia and her mother, regarding the 'clothes show' as a kind of competition between the two families. This behaviour highlights how, as Paul Ginsborg observes, in contemporary Italy there are not enough children to fulfil the emotional needs of the adults.

Nanni and Silvia bring up little Pietro according to the rules first formulated by Benjamin Spock in his famous book, *The Common Sense Book of Baby and Child Care* (1946), later developed and re-worked numerous times. This study foregrounds the importance of the first months of a child's life, including the inter-uterine period, and particularly of breastfeeding and of building a strong emotional bond between parents and their offspring. Accordingly, Pietro is breastfed, and his parents show him on many occasions how they love each other in order to make him feel secure at home. Yet, whereas Silvia appears to be relaxed and in tune with her maternal role, for Nanni fatherhood initially constitutes a problem. For example, we see him getting in the way of Silvia and her mother as they paint the walls of the child's room. The fact that painting is generally regarded as a masculine task suggests that Silvia at home acts as both man and woman. Unable to help the women, Nanni limits himself to photographing their activities, which on the one hand demonstrates his interest in the preparations, but more importantly shows his redundancy. Later we see him being very nervous about the birth – he suggests to Silvia and to the audience that it might be too much for him to witness the pain resulting from this act and that he might need more support than Silvia. On the whole, it appears as if the stereotypical male and female roles and attitudes are interchanged in Nanni and Silvia's household: the man is often weak, dependent and hysterical; the woman strong, independent and emotionally balanced.

After Pietro's birth, Nanni consults a female psychologist who helps him to define his role as a father, persuading him that in his contacts with the child he 'should reveal himself'. He also asks his own mother how she

Nanni with his real-life son Pietro in *Aprile* (1998)

coped with breastfeeding while working full-time as a teacher, and is taken aback to find out that, when he was a baby, he was sometimes left hungry and crying while his mother was out working. This scene draws attention to two previously discussed features of Italian family life: the immense burden of work and responsibility placed on Italian women, particularly those who combine professional careers with motherhood, and the special relationship between Italian mothers and their sons. It appears that even Moretti, who in his earlier films provided us with the scathing criticism of filial love Italian-style, also expects his mother to be little short of a saint; or, perhaps, the ironic tone of the episode suggests that Nanni has more understanding and lower expectations of mothers than his previous cinematic embodiments. Moreover, unlike the male protagonists in the earlier films, Nanni in *Aprile* is not represented as a victim of parental mistakes, and he does not take revenge on the outside world for the real or imaginary sins of his family. On the contrary, it appears that the loving and relaxed relationship between him and his mother is an important factor in his affirmation of life. Similarly, one gets the impression that this relationship serves him as a model for bringing up his own child. Interestingly, the issue of combining parenthood with professional work barely appears in *Aprile* in relation to Silvia. We never learn if, after having had her child, she managed to pursue her earlier career, or what else she did apart from being a mother. Shortly after giving birth Silvia first becomes mute and then virtually disappears from sight, as if her maternal role was taken for granted by the author of *Aprile*. By contrast, Nanni's difficulties with juggling the duties of being a father and a film director fill a substantial portion of the screen time.

The whole issue of bringing up Pietro seems to be isolated from any socio-economic context of parenting in contemporary Italy. It can be argued that this partly results from the relative affluence enjoyed by the parents of little Pietro (the symbol of which is their tasteful penthouse apartment with a huge balcony full of plants), which allows them to concentrate on their child's emotional needs, rather than have to struggle to fulfil his more basic requirements. It could also result from the director's desire not to undermine the happy tone of the film by references to more prosaic and contentious issues, such as the division of housework between men and women in contemporary Italy, or the state provision for helping parents to bring up their children (which was mentioned by Nanni in the 'Hyde Park' episode of *Dear Diary*).

The way in which Moretti represents his character's attitude to parenthood confirms the view that, as Ginsborg puts it, in Italy in the 1990s 'young fathers were more involved with their small children than ever before, both in terms of play and affection' (Ginsborg 2001: 77). Ginsborg also claims that 'the ground rules had been rewritten, but no one was sure of the new text … Nearly always [men] found great difficulty in being *fathers*, behaving more like elder brothers to their children, or friends and confidants or even servants' (ibid.). We argue that this is not true in

Nanni's case. In spite of his encounters with the psychologist and his self-deprecating comments, he comes across as a man completely at ease and happy with his role as a father, even enjoying his fatherly vulnerability. The overall tone of *Aprile* with reference to family is jubilant and it appears that the main function of the mild irony and self-mockery is to prevent the film from becoming too sentimental and simplistic in its celebration of 'family values' and of 'new fatherhood'. Moreover, although Moretti seems to agree that the child/parent relationship in Italy is infantilising, he notices more good than bad points in such a situation, claiming that (as was mentioned in the previous chapter) there is beauty and meaning to being an adult with a childish soul. The softness and self-reflexivity of Nanni's 'new man' and 'father' comes across as even more attractive against the backdrop of the macho, right-wing politicians shown in the film, including the prime minister, Silvio Berlusconi, who in a television interview confesses with pride how he told his little son that 'he will stop repairing television sets and start mending the whole of Italy'. These macho men in the eye of Moretti's camera look not only less sympathetic than his own less self-confident character, but ultimately more ridiculous.

In the course of our analysis, we have established that there is a certain trajectory in the development of Moretti's protagonists: from the attempts to find an alternative to the nuclear family, either by being single and autarchic, or by living in a commune; through the search for a perfect family; to the setting up of a real family in *Aprile*. This real family has the potential to become the perfect family that Michele Apicella, Don Giulio, and Nanni in *Dear Diary* were looking for, as we infer from certain changes in Moretti's protagonist, who is now less uptight, more understanding of the limits of human beings, including mothers and fathers, and who approaches fatherhood with a childish and joyful attitude, despite his many insecurities and doubts.

The following film *The Son's Room* takes this perfect family, which in *Aprile* was only being formed, and that now seems as solid as a rock, and tests its strength and health by inflicting on it a dreadful tragedy. The family consists of the parents, who are both professionals in their forties (the father, Giovanni, is a consultant psychoanalyst, the wife, Paola, owns an upmarket bookshop), and two teenage children: Andrea and Irene, who are both in secondary school. The parents both look attractive and, in spite of presumably being married for more than fifteen years, love each other deeply, as shown in an early scene when they have passionate sex. They also have a healthy and relaxed attitude to their children. The father often jogs with his son, and they all attend sport events, in which the children take part: tennis in the case of Andrea, and volleyball in the case of Irene. We also see meals being prepared by Giovanni (who in this way testifies to his 'new man' credentials) and eaten together by the whole family. Perhaps the best indication of familial love and trust is the fact that, after lying for some time, Andrea finally confesses to his mother that he stole a fossil from the school collection together with a friend. Deborah Young even claims that in *The Son's Room* 'we are presented with one of the happiest families in screen history ... Their harmony at the breakfast table makes the Cleaver family look dysfunctional' (Young 2002b: 14). It is also worth adding that, while Giovanni is played by Moretti, Paola is played by Laura Morante, who was both Silvia in *Sogni d'oro* and Bianca in the eponymous film; something which reinforces the impression that Moretti's protagonist eventually found what he was always looking for – an ideal woman who gave him wonderful children. Furthermore, Giovanni is Moretti's real name, a fact that encourages us to place the film in the same group of films as *Dear Diary* and *Aprile*, and that shows once again that Moretti's protagonist is forever the same character, who is a mix of autobiographical and fictional elements, and who can be seen either synchronically in different phases of his development or, diachronically, in different and parallel incarnations.

The family's harmony is destroyed by Andrea's accidental death while scuba diving with his friends. On that Sunday morning, father and son had planned to go running together, but Giovanni was persuaded by a patient with suicidal tendencies to visit him at home. The rest of the narrative is filled with Giovanni, Paola and Irene's attempts to come to terms with this tragedy, one which is particularly hard to endure as the family is secular and for them putting Andrea in a coffin is the final stage of their life together. From our perspective, it is important to draw attention to the different ways in which Giovanni on the one hand, and Paola and Irene on the other, react to Andrea's death. The grieving Giovanni is placed at the centre of the director's attention. As Philip Kemp observes, 'while both women externalise their grief, Giovanni closes his away, letting it poison his relations with his family and his patients. In some of the film's most desolate scenes we see him obsessively re-running the events of the fateful day as they might have been had he put off his importunate patient and kept his promise to his son, eroding himself with futile guilt' (Kemp 2002: 56).

With his internalisation of suffering and inability to 'move on', or at least salvage something positive from the memories of a happy past, Giovanni is similar to some male characters in earlier films by Moretti, particularly Michele in *Sogni d'oro* and *Bianca*, who also seemed to accept the inevitability and necessity of suffering, and the impossibility of happiness. Moreover, it appears as if there is only a thin line between Giovanni's mourning and madness. A sign of this is his decision to quit his job, because, as he puts it, 'he is losing his objectivity', a state which is marked by his inability to have a neutral, serene attitude towards his patients.

Yet ultimately the differences between Giovanni on the one hand and Michele in *Sogni d'oro* and *Bianca* on the other are greater than their similarities. In the end Giovanni begins to overcome his trauma and to become reconciled with reality, whereas Michele in the previously mentioned films sinks even further into madness and locks himself in the past. A crucial factor in Giovanni's ability to heal the terrible wounds caused by his son's death is the help offered to him by the women who surround him: his wife, his daughter and especially his son's ex-girlfriend, Arianna. The visit of Arianna, who is accompanied by her new boyfriend, Stefano, makes Giovanni take an interest in something beyond his own grief. This change is marked by his decision to give Arianna and Stefano a lift to France, when it emerges that they planned to hitchhike there. Giovanni, Irene and Paola first accompany Arianna and Stefano to a service station on the motorway, but rather than dropping them off there they decide to take them to the border with France, travelling for the whole night. This trip draws Giovanni and Paola close once again, both in the physical sense of sharing the confinement of their car, and in the sense of being emotionally close, of sharing thoughts and feelings, something which had not been possible since Andrea's death. This possibility of and need for marital closeness is revealed in a simple scene, in which Giovanni asks Paola not to fall asleep in the car, but to talk to him and keep him company. In the morning Giovanni, Paola and Irene stroll on a beach. As Philip Kemp observes: 'There are no hugs or effusions of love; the three walk apart, but there is a sense that a burden may be lifting. (Quite literally they have crossed a border; the past is another country.) It is a subtle, wistful closure: Moretti holds out the possibility of grief fading and lives repairing themselves, but he is too honest to offer us more than that' (Kemp 2002: 56).

In contrast to the 'Apicella films', and despite the sombre tone of most of the film, the story depicted in *The Son's Room* is not unhappy, because the main character does not rupture his connection with reality, seeking refuge from human imperfections and from fate's cruelty in solitude and madness, but is eventually prepared to face the world. Similarly, although the family here is a cause of immense human suffering, it is also the main source of hope and reason to live. This message about the importance, even necessity, of having a (traditional) family is most striking in the episodes of Giovanni's work as a psychoanalyst. The majority of his patients live on their own, or in non-traditional households, suggesting that there is a link between lack of family and mental dysfunction. Take, for example, the suicidal man whose condition appears to have much to do with the fact that he has nobody with whom to share his distressing experiences. In some cases, the source of mental problems is the very inability of a patient to conform to a traditional family model, as in the case of a woman who suffers deeply because she and her husband cannot have children. Giovanni is portrayed almost as a substitute parent to his patients; somebody who knows more about life than 'his children', but cannot give them any precise recipes for leading a healthy and happy existence. His role as a surrogate parent is most visible in the scenes when he informs them about quitting his job and consequently that their therapy with him has come to an end. Many patients feel betrayed by him as if they had been abandoned by a parent. The fact that Giovanni has his office in his own house not only strengthens his image as parent to his patients, but also increases the contrast between the happiness and the normality of his private life and the misery and pathology of his patients' existence. The difference remains valid even after Andrea's death; although at this stage Giovanni is deeply unhappy, he is still more in control of his own life than are the people whom he counsels.

The choice of Giovanni's profession also allows Moretti to 'revisit' many of the problems that affected the male protagonists in his earlier films: aggression, schizophrenia, neurosis, sexual frustration, pathological shyness and loneliness. Subscribing to the idea that Giovanni is the last link in the transformation of Moretti's alter ego, his last incarnation, then we may argue that not only did he mature and become able to have a family of his own, but even to help other people. Obviously the death of Giovanni's son changed his position both in relation to his own family and to other people. Yet he is not responsible for that tragedy and the fact that he is able to survive it in spite of the immense pain caused by losing his son (which in itself is a sign of his love for his child, and accordingly, of the soundness of his family) is testimony to the health and robustness of his personality. Giovanni is able to survive what would certainly destroy most if not all of his fore-runners in Moretti's earlier films.

The sombre tone and lack of comical or ironical scenes suggest that in this film Moretti came to certain conclusions regarding the issues therein represented, and particularly the family, rather than treating them with the ambivalence characteristic of earlier films. It is reasonable to assume that family in *The Son's Room* is as endorsed by Moretti as it is by Giovanni. Even the motif of Andrea's room, which remains unchanged after his death, and is invested of additional prominence by providing the title of the film, alludes to the sacredness and durability of the institution of the family.

Conclusion

In terms of depicting the family, Moretti does not fit the commonly held view of him (supported in other chapters of this book) as a rebellious artist who opposes and castigates Italian mores and values. On the contrary, in this respect he appears to be a traditional Italian through and through. This is revealed by the persistence of the motif of family life – in his films, families are not only represented, but also thoroughly discussed and assessed. The very fact that Moretti includes his own family in *Aprile*, one of his most 'pro-family' films, is evidence of the significance of this institution for Moretti, and of his positive attitude towards it. Nevertheless, as demonstrated by his early films, Moretti criticises heavily certain family arrangements and structures, which have been, and in many cases still are, favoured by Italians. The role of the father in the patriarchal family is especially criticised and seen as the source of much misery for the family. On the other hand, in none of his films do we find a vigorous denunciation of this institution, nor a viable alternative to it. Moreover, as time passes, a growing emphasis is placed on the importance of having a family in order to be happy and even to remain mentally healthy. It is by no means an unreasonable assertion that the pursuit of having a 'perfect family' – which at a certain stage simply comes to mean a 'normal family' – is the main quest for Moretti's males. This is particularly striking in the light of the opinion, conveyed in this chapter, that we live in a time in which patriarchy (in its classical sense) and the traditional family are gradually disappearing in the Western world.

CHAPTER THREE

Laughing Through the Tears: Tragicomedy and Existential Irony

Irony is no joke.
       – Friedrich Schlegel

Without irony, one becomes ridiculous.
       – Nanni Moretti

Humour is the most important tool that Moretti uses in his films to criticise and comment on society, on politics, on life in contemporary Italy and in the Western world in general, as well as on his own persona. Moretti creates his own type of humour, a singular mix of witticism, satire, parody and grotesque laughter, which is often juxtaposed with a tragic element. In this chapter, we argue that Moretti's comedy is best viewed as a form of tragicomedy, and we analyse some of its components, its workings, as well as its limits. We also discuss the film-maker's selection of irony as his prevalent approach to life, a position that we term existential irony, and that we define by bringing into play the writings of Sören Kierkegaard. To begin with, though, we are going to situate Moretti's cinema within the context of the Italian comedy, looking in particular at its relationship with, as well as its criticism of, the tradition of the *commedia all'italiana* (comedy Italian-style), the genre that was born at the end of the 1950s and traversed at least twenty years of national cinema. Furthermore, we will discuss the affinity of Moretti's comedy with that of another contemporary director to whom he has often been compared: Woody Allen.

Comedy Moretti-style

When he made his debut on the scene of Italian cinema with *Io sono un autarchico* and then with *Ecce Bombo*, Moretti was called a 'young comedian' by the critics, a label that was soon attached to a series of authors each of whom made his first film not long after Moretti: Francesco Nuti, Maurizio Nichetti, Roberto Benigni, Carlo Verdone and Massimo Troisi. By using the expression 'young comedians' the critics conveyed the sense of the emergence of a new school from the ashes of the old one. As the years passed, it became clear that these 'young' directors had very little in common, in terms of style, approach to comedy and artistic ambition. The expression 'young comedians' was also meant to indicate both continuity between the previous generation of directors of *commedia all'italiana*, and a break with it. In an essay on Italian comedy of the 1980s, Giulio Marlia set out to explore the relationship between the two generations of comedians. In agreement with most critics, he identified the principal characteristic of *commedia all'italiana* as its relationship to reality: Italian cinema from the end of the war to the 1970s laughed 'about and against reality, social reality in particular' (Marlia 1988: 99) and 'was characterised by the presence of more or less robust doses of realism, of spirit of observation and, at times, of criticism of the social, political and sexual mores of Italians' (1988: 101). Marlia thus asked whether the 'young comedians' continue or break with this tradition, and concluded that, on the one hand, there is in their work a clear absence of explicit references to the current socio-political reality (then dominated by terrorism, unemployment, political scandals and an increasing lack of political commitment), but that, on the other hand, they are the product of their times, the 'sons of the reflux', who reflect how 'unengaged, individualistic, confused and uncertain' (1988: 103) the whole of Italian society has become.

Whereas it is true that most of Moretti's early films (those widely described as 'comedies') do not engage directly with terrorism or political scandals, they do offer criticism of current ways of thinking, of family structures, sexual mores, political opinions, mainstream as well as avant-garde art and other current issues, as we have shown in the preceding chapters. Marlia himself recognised that Moretti, 'of the whole group of the new comedians, is surely the most "committed" one' (1988: 107). The presence of commitment to depicting and analysing a socio-politic reality seems to indicate continuity rather than a break with the tradition of the *commedia all'italiana*; even so, the young director immediately refused to be identified with the Italian comedy, to the extent of even disparaging and criticising it overtly in his first films. In *Io sono un autarchico*, a friend of Michele announces him that film-maker Lina Wertmüller was offered a professorship at Berkeley, and Michele reacts by spitting green foam from his mouth – a reaction that reveals his disgust and perhaps even his envy. In *Ecce Bombo* Michele criticises a symbol of Italian comedy, actor Nino Manfredi, for advertising brands of cigarettes in his films, and attacks another icon of that type of cinema, Alberto Sordi, when he shouts at a man whom he accuses of having clichéd opinions that he 'thinks he is in an Alberto Sordi film', and that he 'deserves' the actor.

Numerous Italian critics, particularly during the first years of his career, have engaged with the question of whether Moretti is to be placed within the tradition of the *commedia all'italiana* or outside it, without reaching a consensus. Some have highlighted how the *commedia all'italiana* was a genre, whereas Moretti's cinema defies categories and rules. The *commedia all'italiana* was based on the stardom of a small group of actors (Gassman, Sordi, Tognazzi, Manfredi), as well as on the exploitation of a certain number of standard situations and of 'types' rather than characters, which in the end fossilised into sterile stereotypes. Other critics highlighted the traditional type of narrative preferred by the authors of the *commedia all'italiana*, which is completely avoided in Moretti's films. Some critics, on the other hand, believed that Moretti either renovated (Masi 1984) or simply repeated the stereotypes of the Italian comedy (Fofi 1990), even if in disguise (Escobar 1978).

Moretti's abhorrence for the *commedia all'italiana* may be seen as partly generational (in the sense of a reaction against the cinema of the fathers), but it is principally ideological and stylistic, as confirmed respectively by the two following quotations:

The films that are widely regarded as the best Italian comedies are those in which the directors did not describe themselves but – sometimes with affection, other times with racism – social categories that were distant from them: the under-proletariat, the proletariat aspiring to turn into small bourgeoisie ... Much *commedia all'italiana* was based on the scorn of the tacky ornament. In the cinema as well as in life, I am on the side of those who keep the cellophane on the chairs in order to spare them, of those who have tacky ornaments in their houses, and I truly am not able to mock them. I am interested in the opposite operation ... to describe, and to mock, a group that is homogeneous with me (from a social, generational and political viewpoint), if not even myself. (Moretti quoted in De Bernardinis 1998: 6)

I like a type of comedy that subtracts. My type of comedy does not overdo things. [*Moretti places crockery, glasses, ashtrays in a pile and says, 'This is traditional Italian comedy, putting everything in and overdoing things.' After dispersing the objects, he proclaims, 'This is my comedy.'*] (Moretti quoted in Porton & Ellickson 1995: 14)

We suggest that the main factors that allow us to distinguish Moretti's cinema from the *commedia all'italiana* are the targets of the humour and the type of humour he creates. As Moretti indicated in the quotation above, the target of his humour is not a social class which is seen as inferior to the director, but the director himself, his social class and his milieu. As a critic has written, Moretti is the opposite of the comedy represented by Alberto Sordi because 'Sordi, his bravura apart, is an incarnation of a facile way to satirise society, choosing as the target an average, an ordinary Italian who does not belong to anybody ... Moretti never alludes to an average type, but shoots real social groups and real people, beginning with himself' (Papuzzi 1999: 81–2). As regards the type of humour created by Moretti, as early as 1977 Mino Argentieri had already noticed that: 'Nothing [like the *commedia all'italiana*] is more distant from *Io sono un autarchico*, a film which is nourished by a humour of provocative effects and of cold and intellectual roots, disenchanted, reflexive and sad in its irony, thus able to penetrate deeply into the current custom and into today's discontents' (Argentieri 1990: 133). We agree with Argentieri that the most distinctive component of Moretti's humour is its 'disenchanted, reflexive and sad' irony, which contrasts rather strongly with the type of humour promoted by most *commedia all'italiana* and that can be more appropriately described as derisive, as seeking the complicity of the audience, and at times even as coarse.

The debate on Moretti's links with the *commedia all'italiana* subsided over the years, when it became clear that the director could not simply be seen as a comedian, and that his films had a strong dramatic component. In truth, Moretti always drew attention to this, as can be seen in the following remarks:

> I really did not expect such a reception and success for *Ecce Bombo*. I thought it was a dramatic and a rather partial film. Instead it was taken for a comedy, and for a film about the whole young generation, whereas I thought I had made a film about a section of it. (Moretti quoted in De Bernardinis 1998: 3)

> I have always made dramatic films ... Up to now, being considered as an author of comedies has been useful to me in continuing my work. But the dramatic, sorrowful and melancholic zones of my films, I think, have been underestimated. (Moretti quoted in Masi 1984: 49)

Moretti's comedy has also been often associated by critics to that of Woody Allen, another director who is the protagonist or one of the characters in many of his own films. Like Allen, Moretti is an 'author and director of comedies, a hyper-narcissistic actor/character with an over-inflated tendency to introspection, verbal excess and analysis of self and others' (Philippon 1985: 49). Allen, of course, comes from a very different socio-cultural background, which constitutes the greatest difference between the two authors. Nevertheless, both directors concentrate their irony on themselves and their environment, and employ a similar mix of wit, satire, parody, grotesque laughter, and a tragic sense of solitude, inadequacy and loss. Cremonini transcribed a monologue from *Ecce Bombo* that, as the critic writes, 'looks like the Italian version of a Woody Allen monologue' (Cremonini 1999: 42):

> I should have been born 100 years ago, in 1848. The barricades in Leipzig. At twenty-two I would have already done the Commune

in Paris. Now: state employee, with my colleagues who spend their holidays following all the festivals of the Communist Party, with the dancers from Moldavia and the girls imported from Hungary. Gino Paoli, Pinocchio, Mike Bongiorno, Marilyn Monroe, Altafini, Gianni Morandi, Gianni Rivera all had a function in the Sixties. What are we doing? What is happening? When will we see the sun? I am sick. I even feel cold. (*Ecce Bombo*)

The affinity with Allen's humour is evident. Not only is this type of verbal humour reminiscent of Woody Allen, but so also are certain episodes, especially in Moretti's early films. In particular, flashbacks to the authors' childhoods, as in Moretti's *Palombella rossa* and in Allen's *Stardust Memories* and *Zelig*, are characterised by an absurd vein and have much in common visually, despite the cultural and geographical distance between the two authors. Both directors as children are portrayed as small versions of their adult selves, already excluded from society and chastised by others. Similarly, in the portrayal of their families, the male, father-like figures are often depicted as ineffective and pathetic, while women are usually painted with more affection.

Another author whom we feel has some affinity with Moretti is Chaplin, as he also split himself in two, and from the outside observed himself as lonely, different and defeated in the world. Although the dissimilarities

Michele (Nanni Moretti) eating from an oversized Nutella jar in *Bianca* (1983)

between the two are much more numerous than the similarities, both Charlot and Michele Apicella are figures of our inadequacy, of our being at odds with the world, and both suffer from their solitude, ineffectiveness and exclusion. Nevertheless, as Alberto Moravia noted, whereas Chaplin's comedy is directly linked with the reality of life, Moretti's comedy, like Woody Allen's, is somehow filtered by the contemporary mass media culture (Moravia 1990: 158). Thus, whereas Chaplin is a modern author, whose films are a commentary on generalised human experiences (love, work, poverty, fatherhood), Moretti is a postmodern film-maker, whose work deals with a fragmented world and reflects the kaleidoscopic nature of the many discourses of our society.

In the next section, we intend to show how the 'dramatic, sorrowful and melancholic zones' of Moretti's films, combined with their witty, satirical and grotesque zones, produce what we will call Moretti's tragicomedy.

Moretti's tragicomedy

Mixed terms like 'dark comedy', 'tragicomedy' and 'comical satire' testify to 'the profound difficulty of demarcation between the tragic and the comic temper' (Merchant 1972: 40). Without wishing to put forward generalised conclusions on humour and on comedy, fields of inquiry which are notoriously impervious to analysis, in this chapter by the term tragicomedy – 'a category with a consistent history of critical usage' since the time of Plautus (Merchant 1972: 39) – we mean the co-presence of tears and laughter, expressions of apparently irreconcilable emotions.

It is clear why Moretti's films cannot be straightforwardly called 'comedies'. If we take a broad definition of comedy, such as that found in a dictionary – 'Stage-play of light, amusing and often satirical character, chiefly representing everyday life, and with happy ending' (quoted in Neale and Krutnik 1990: 11) – we instantly know that Moretti's films are excluded from this category, since they do not have happy endings, and provoke not only laughter and amusement, but also sadness and melancholy, anger and sorrow.

These mixed feelings are present in Moretti's work on two levels. The first, and more immediate, is that of an irony that looks in a 'disenchanted, reflexive and sad' manner at contemporary society and its shortcomings: the decline of political engagement; the loss of solid values; the spread of conventional opinions; the corruption of language and the use of clichéd expressions; the lack of rigour and integrity in the press; the inefficiency of the Italian left; the rise of an undemocratic political power in contemporary Italy – all are objectives of Moretti's satirical attacks and can be described as a laughing through the tears. We will devote a later section of this chapter to a discussion of Moretti's satire and of the objects of his criticism.

On a second level, Moretti's films are tragicomic because laughter in them is rarely jovial, and on the contrary often presents a dark side. To take an early example, the theatre scenes of *Io sono un autarchico* – on the one hand we laugh at the clumsy acting and the naive symbolism of the performance, on the other hand we feel sorry when the audience refuses to engage in the debate solicited by the director, as well as when the actors part at the end of the show, and their experience seems to end in nothing. This laughter, which is connected with the inadequacy of human beings, and which mixes with a sense of pity for them, could be ascribed to the tradition of humour represented by authors such as Miguel de Cervantes and Alessandro Manzoni: a humour that derives from an understanding of the facts of life, that regards people with a humane and sympathetic gaze, and which produces a laughter that is not caustic (as in satire) nor scoffing (as in a grotesque representation), but rather compassionate. Moretti surely looks at his young characters in *Io sono un autarchico* and *Ecce Bombo* with a modicum of this type of humour – he simultaneously laughs at them and pities them. Nevertheless, the presence of this 'humanistic' humour in Moretti is not enough to explain the extreme sadness caused by his films – this is, on the contrary, produced by the presence of zones that function as borders or limits of the comedy. We refer to elements such as the character of schizophrenic Olga in *Ecce Bombo*; the moments of misery and humiliation of the director in *Sogni d'oro*, as well as his final transformation into a werewolf; the murderous madness of the protagonist of *Bianca* and his final remark that 'it is sad to die without children'; the suicide of the mother and the suffering characters that populate *La messa è finita*; the car accident that closes *Palombella rossa*; the experience of cancer in *Dear Diary*; the fear of becoming old in *Aprile*; the death of the protagonist's son and the mourning in *The Son's Room*.

Loss and death, though, are more than just the limits of the comedy, they are also its source. As Piera Detassis noticed, Moretti's 'harrowing comedy' is born 'from inadequacy, from loss' (quoted in Cremonini 1999: 40). For his part, Giorgio Cremonini suggests that solitude, seen as separation from the *other*, is the source of the tragic feelings in Moretti. As we have seen earlier in the chapter devoted to family, Moretti's main character has a strong nostalgia for his childhood and, even in adulthood, continues to suffer from his separation from the mother, which psychoanalysis has recognised to be at the origin of the human feelings of loss and incompleteness: 'Solitude is separation of the *self* from the *other*, an opposition that comedy does not solve in a dialectic manner, but as a defeat, as a contrast which is destined to survive every *false* integration' (Cremonini 1999: 41). This defeat, though, is not supinely accepted. For Cremonini, even the most melancholic moments of Moretti's cinema are characterised by an attitude, which produces comedy, to unveil 'that which is absurd, incongruous and perturbing in the *other*, with whom the subject has to deal' (1999: 39).

What is truly tragic in this form of comedy is that the *other* is, of course, always also our *self*. As Lacan has proposed through his theory of the mirror phase, we learn to recognise ourselves as independent human beings in a mirror image that is primarily *other*, a double. This almost schizophrenic experience of the formation of the self is re-presented in the work of the director who is also the protagonist of his films. The film-maker scrutinises his own self, which is both the source of the directorial gaze and the object of observation, schizophrenically divided between the observing viewpoint and the observed object. We suggest that this is the reason why the activity of making films is experienced as misery and anguish in *Sogni d'oro*: the film-maker Michele Apicella clearly suffers while writing and then shooting his film, and tries to dissuade his assistants from wanting to become directors; at the end of the film he even transforms into a werewolf, revealing the split in his personality. A similar split emerges in the teacher protagonist of *Bianca*, who lives a double life, *à la* Dr Jekyll and Mr Hyde and, perhaps less overtly but equally tragically, in all Moretti's protagonists who are divided between adulthood and childhood. Moretti not only looks at himself from the outside, but also satirises himself and his personality, which is split into a deriding will and a derided object. In interviews, Moretti often suggested that for him 'comedy was a way of exorcising the weight of autobiography, because if one does autobiography and takes himself seriously, one risks becoming ridiculous' (Moretti quoted in Detassis 1986b: 48). Thus we could say that comedy is what comes between one's self and his own portrait (or double), and its tragic component is the consciousness of the irreparable split between the two.

One of the mechanisms sometimes used by Moretti to provoke laughter in his films is the grotesque. Examples of this repeated presence are the oversized objects, looking unnatural and absurd, such as the huge jar of chocolate spread that appears in *Bianca* and the gigantic joint smoked by Nanni in *Aprile*; and also the disguise, a classical reference to the double and the carnival, as in the werewolf makeup worn in *Bianca* and the animal-like costume worn by Michele in the TV contest in *Sogni d'oro*. Other elements cannot perhaps be rigorously classified as grotesque, but are nevertheless absurd emblems, for instance evidently artificial props, like the paper-pulp sun that rises at the end of *Palombella rossa*. These elements are all indicative of Moretti's tragicomic sense of life – they signify life's dark and absurd side, and ultimately the presence of death.

Satire and its discontents

Satire differs radically from the type of 'humanistic comedy' that we have described above. Whereas the latter looks with sympathy and compassion at the world, the former involves indignation, anger and annoyance with it. Satire and comedy are very different if we are to agree with A. E. Dyson that 'satire judges man against an ideal, while comedy sets him against a norm … The two modes then of satire and comedy would seem to oppose bitter glee and compassionate laughter, destructive judgement and an urbane certainty of redemption' (quoted in Merchant 1972: 42). These two different types of laughter, nevertheless, can coexist in the same work. They do so in Moretti, who is capable both of a sympathetic and of a caustic view. In the course of our analysis, we will also occasionally refer to another comic form: parody. In strict terms, parody is a mode of comedy that draws upon generic conventions in order to produce laughter, and it is to be distinguished from satire: 'Satire is often confused with parody, but the two are quite different. Where parody … draws on – and highlights – aesthetic conventions, satire draws – and highlights – social ones' (Neale & Krutnik 1990: 19). To date, only once has Moretti used parody as the supporting structure of a film (the early Super-8 short *Come parli frate?*, a parody of a major work of Italian literature, Alessandro Manzoni's *I promessi sposi*), but exploited this form several times in his main features as a vehicle for his satire – examples, which will be illustrated below, are the parody of trash television in *Sogni d'oro* and that of a contemporary Italian film in *Dear Diary*. In *Come parli frate?*, as Flavio De Bernardini has suggested, the parody no longer refers to the characters of the novel, but to the mythical dimension reached by those characters (De Bernardinis 2001: 40–1); the film, for Alessandro Cappabianca, constructs the parody along the lines of Manzoni's irony, and founds it on the principle of contamination – for instance, borrowing from the conventions of the western, or constructing a character on different and contrasting models (Cappabianca 1990).

The objects of Moretti's satire are many and diverse. The first are his persona and his milieu. In *Io sono un autarchico* and *Ecce Bombo*, as well as in some of the previous shorts, Moretti made fun of himself as a member of a certain social group – the young, left-wing and bourgeois Italian (or, more specifically, Roman) generation born in the 1950s, the generation that came of age during the 1970s, the years of terrorism, and that lived in the phase of the disillusionment with political engagement. The anxieties of the young militants and the shortcomings of the Communist project are satirised, for instance, in the short *La sconfitta* (literally, 'the defeat') in which Luciano (Moretti) asks a party leader, who is giving him a lesson made up of formulaic phrases, when the passage from capitalism to communism will finally take place, and if he will be able at least to see a bit of the transitional phase (this sequence is also used as a flashback in *Palombella rossa*). In *Io sono un autarchico* Moretti again satirises his activism and that of his friends and his generation and, more specifically, certain stereotypes of militancy ('I don't understand why one should feel more left-wing if he wears an earring and has only two potatoes for dinner...' 'Who said that that means being more left-wing?' 'Yes, but why then do I feel more right-wing!'); his own limitations as well as the obscurity of political language (Michele reads a difficult piece and exclaims: 'I can't understand anything! Perhaps I should have chosen a different ideology'); the ephemeral character of political activism ('Do you remember when we all used to talk about Ireland? Who remembers about Ireland anymore?'); as well as the shortcomings of the leadership of the Italian Communist Party ('20,000 extra memberships for our party this year – as if they were memberships of the Roma football team!').

Moretti's persona is also criticised from other perspectives. In *Io sono un autarchico*, *Ecce Bombo* and *Sogni d'oro*, for instance, the film-maker paints himself as critical of contemporary Italian cinema, but also admits to being motivated by a dose of envy for the success of others. In the first film, he lets his friend Fabio accuse him precisely of this after listening to Michele's tirade against Italian critics and films; in *Ecce Bombo* he mocks his girlfriend for her involvement with what he regards as low-level film-making, but also seems jealous of her activity; in *Sogni d'oro* film-maker Michele despises his colleague and rival Gigio Cimino, but clearly resents the latter's ability to make a light entertainment film that also has a political slant. In *Sogni d'oro*, Michele's rage towards his rival and his contempt for the audience is not only satirised, but also punished through the humiliation that Moretti inflicts on Michele in a grotesque television contest. Another, and connected, aspect of his own personality that Moretti mocks, particularly in his first films, is vanity – as when he asks his girlfriend in *Ecce Bombo* if she is crying because he is 'a great artist' (although he never produces anything artistic); or when, in the same film, he wonders whether people would notice him more if he went to a party and then stayed by himself, or rather if he did not go at all. His vanity seems to be also connected to the belief that all women should inevitably fall in love with him – a belief that of course hides Michele's inability to relate to the other sex, a characteristic that emerges more and more clearly in *Sogni d'oro* and in *Bianca*. His awkwardness in romantic and sexual matters is also represented by the recurrent joke of his fondness for sweets and cakes, which work as a replacement gratification, a joke that often possesses a grotesque component.

As we have already discussed in the chapter on family, Moretti also satirises his own (and his generation's) difficulty in detaching himself from the protective embrace of the family, and particularly of the mother: comical scenes on this topic can be found for instance in *Io sono un autarchico*, in which one of the friends continuously talks of leaving home, but claims that his parents do not want to let him go, until they eventually throw him out; and in *Sogni d'oro*, when Michele tries unskilfully to pack his suitcase and then lets his mother do it for him. Satirical scenes about his attachment to his mother recur in Moretti's films – even in recent ones, in which he seems more 'adult' and independent. In *Palombella rossa* Michele, in a moment of despair, cries, 'Mum, come and get me!'; in *Aprile* Nanni asks his (real) mother how she could have breastfed him and worked as a teacher at the same time, and feels very sorry for himself when she answers that sometimes he was left hungry waiting for her. Another aspect of his private life that Moretti criticises is the contrast between his own ideal of a perfect couple and a perfect family, and his inability to achieve one. The feeling of inadequacy at times becomes very bitter and devoid of humour – as happens in the saddest moments of *Bianca*, or of *La messa è finita*.

As we have seen, Moretti mocks himself both as an individual and as a member and representative of a specific social group. On more than one occasion, the film-maker has declared that 'I make fun of my own milieu because I think that when you make fun of yourself, you have more of a right to make fun of others' (Moretti quoted in Porton & Ellickson 1995: 14). After criticising for years the bourgeois left-wing community and the Italian Communist Party in his films, in *Palombella rossa* and in *Aprile* Moretti includes overt criticism of the 'others', the political opponents. In *Palombella rossa* the most specific figure of political satire is that of the Catholic who keeps harassing Michele, telling him that he himself and the Communist MP 'have much in common', that they 'are the same', and trying to persuade him to listen to his own, new age-type spiritual leader. Whereas *Palombella rossa* still mainly focuses on the criticism of PCI, *Aprile* overtly attacks the political opponents, and in particular Silvio Berlusconi, media tycoon and newly-elected prime minister; the ex-Fascist Party, Alleanza Nazionale; Emilio Fede, director of news on one of Berlusconi's channels; and Umberto Bossi, leader of the separatist Northern League. The film opens on the night of 28 March 1994, the day of the general election, won by the centre-right coalition led by Berlusconi. Nanni and his mother are watching television, and the images alternate with comments from Nanni. First we see Emilio Fede claiming that Berlusconi won the election despite having most of the press against him (a rather paradoxical statement, seeing that he owned three major national television channels, as well as national newspapers and weekly magazines); then we are shown the headquarters of PDS (the ex-Communist Party), where the leaders fail to show up and talk to the journalists (and Nanni comments disapprovingly); finally we see Berlusconi who tells how his child at school, having been asked what his daddy did for a living, replied that he mended televisions – Berlusconi suggests that he will now have to mend Italy itself. Nanni does not comment, but smokes a joint instead, the first of his life, as he emphasises. Satire here hits both left-wing and right-wing parties. Whereas the leaders of PDS are accused of absenteeism (and Nanni jokes: 'Since we always lost, why should it be different this time?'), Berlusconi's and Fede's words do not need any comment – the joke of the joint is enough to make Nanni's opinion quite clear. This gag works on the level of the grotesque and of the absurd: in fact, the joint is grotesquely oversized, suggesting the great need for oblivion in the face of the victory of the right; secondly, the absurdity of the situation is produced by the impassibility of Nanni's mother, and by Nanni's monologue, which switches from the present to the past, and from fiction to comment: 'That night I smoked a joint. It was the first of my life.'

Political satire is pervasive in *Aprile*, and is also directed at the world of the Italian press. Nanni accuses journalists of writing for newspapers and magazines belonging to conflicting political areas, thus of being unreliable and dishonest, and the leftist weekly *L'Espresso* is accused of putting naked women on the front cover to attract more sales. In one of the most incisive satirical scenes of *Aprile*, Nanni, who has glued together a vast number of newspaper clippings that he kept over the years, rolls himself in the resulting gigantic sheet, commenting that all newspapers in Italy are the same, thus that readers have at their disposal only one newspaper to read.

The press was also an object of Moretti's satire in several earlier films. In *Io sono un autarchico* Michele suggests with a sneer that half of the Italian intellectuals write in pornographic magazines, and accuses film critics of inviting the audience to go to see appalling films; real-life critic Beniamino Placido plays the role of a theatre critic, and through him Moretti satirises the obscure language of reviewers and their intellectual snobbishness. In *Ecce Bombo* we are regularly shown the crew of a local television channel, Tele California, which claims to report originally and accurately on youth culture, whereas it only repeats clichéd views of young people. In the same film, the experience of the independent radio (*radio libere*) of the 1970s is looked at with more sympathy, even if also in this case it seems that the medium is not used in a truly effective way and the communication established with the audience is inconsequential. In *Sogni d'oro* Moretti offers a parody of trash television, through the contest between the two young film-makers in a programme which includes a boxing match, an interview about their sexual habits, and a weird competition with the two men dressed as penguins; the satire of mass media in this film reaches its peak when Michele shouts at the audience, 'Shit public!', and the spectators repeat the expression several times like a slogan. In *Palombella rossa* Moretti criticises the language of journalism, its abuse of stereotypical expressions, and its superficiality; the immediate target of the satire is a journalist who comes to the swimming pool to interview Michele, and who is guilty of using corrupted Italian (she uses foreign words like 'trend' and 'cheap'), of stereotypical, empty expressions (such as 'marriage falling apart'), and of superficiality (she admits that she usually writes about sport rather than politics, and more than once consults an abridged history of the Italian Communist Party before asking her stereotypical questions). At one point, Michele gets so upset at her that he slaps her. In *Dear Diary* Moretti once again satirises the language of journalism and the seriousness of film reviewers; this time the object of his criticism is a preposterous film review of John McNaughton's *Henry: Portrait of Serial Killer* (1990), which Nanni found disgusting. For revenge, he imagines himself being at the bedside of the journalist who wrote it, torturing him by reading a selection of passages from his articles. This scene once again displays the absurd vein in Moretti's comedy.

The condemnation of the language of journalism, of which we have seen some examples, is part of a more extensive discourse led by Moretti on the corruption of language in general. As he once jokingly remarked in an interview, 'If there were an Assessor for Language, I would put myself forward as a candidate' (quoted in Comuzio 1993: 63). His protagonists often react with anger at the use that other characters make of improper or corrupt expressions; for instance, Michele in *Ecce Bombo* corrects his mother, who puts an article before the name of a person, a Milanese practice that disturbs Moretti's protagonist. This and similar examples testify to the fondness of the film-maker for the purity of language, not so much per se, but as a symptom of a better way of thinking and, thus, of living. Another aspect of Moretti's criticism of the current use of language relates to the language of authority, something which brings us back to his criticism of politicians, of political discourse, of ideology and of the media.[1] Exponents of authority who are criticised by Moretti are not only politicians or influential critics, but men in general. Masculinity is, in fact, one of the objectives of his criticism and, of course, authority and machismo often go hand in hand. This is true of the personalities mocked in *Aprile* and, in particular, of Silvio Berlusconi, who presents himself as an unpleasant and immodest superman and saviour of the country. Similarly, the macho and self-important image of Umberto Bossi, as well as his bombastic speech, is ridiculed by Moretti's camera. Another category of authority that is criticised by Moretti in the last chapter of *Dear Diary* is that of the doctors. Here the consultants (all men) are represented as self-assured and paternalistic with their patient, but their poise is in reality a façade hiding their ignorance of the nature of Nanni's illness. In order to preserve their position of authority, these men prefer to pretend they are in control, and prescribe inappropriate medicines, rather than admit to their ignorance. Furthermore, it is significant that the only doctor who admits his defeat, and in doing so puts Nanni on the right track, is Chinese, confirming the tendency of Moretti's cinema to pass judgment on certain shortcomings specific to Italian society and the Italian character.

Not only male figures of authority, but also men in general are mocked by Moretti, even if usually with more affection than that shown for those in public life. Some of the most comic moments in Moretti's films are linked to funny male figures, and primarily to Moretti himself. Other laughable figures are, for instance, Fabio, the theatre director in *Io sono un autarchico*; the group of friends in *Ecce Bombo*, and in particular Mirko (played by Fabio Traversa, the actor who also played Fabio in the previous film); Gaetano, the unlucky director in *Sogni d'oro* (played by Alessandro Haber); Gerardo (Renato Carpentieri), Nanni's friend in the episode 'Islands' in *Dear Diary*; and the actor of the musical in *Aprile* (Silvio Orlando). Women are rarely funny or the butt of jokes in the way men are, suggesting that Moretti intends to mock men, or at least certain expressions of masculinity, much more than women and femininity.

Another object of Moretti's satire is the institution of the school, which is also linked to the discourse on authority. References to the Italian scholastic system recur in his films – both Moretti's parents were teachers, thus, as the film-maker once said, 'I always breathed this climate, these problems' (quoted in Giovannini, Magrelli & Sesti 1986: 32). For instance, in *Ecce Bombo* Michele gives grinds to two high-school students, who eventually take their final year exams. The scene set in the exam room is very amusing, the examiners changing the layout of the desks in order to make the students feel at ease, as if for a conversation rather than an interrogation.[2] The funniest moment is when a student presents his research paper on a poet, who is unknown to the examiners, until the poet himself – a young lad with very long hair and punk-looking clothes – comes forward and sits next to the candidate. The clearest articulation of Moretti's discourse on the school is to be found in *Bianca*, in which Michele is a maths teacher dealing with his first job. The school represented in *Bianca* is one of the main sources of laughter in this otherwise very dark and pessimistic film. The Marilyn Monroe School is wholly unusual: the office of the schoolmaster is dominated by a poster of Dean Martin and Jerry Lewis; in the classrooms, the photograph of the president of the Italian Republic is replaced by that of the goalkeeper of the Italian football team; the students have at their disposal a bar with pinball and slot-machines; the history teacher, a favourite of the schoolmaster, lectures on the life of a contemporary Italian songwriter, using the jukebox in the classroom as teaching support; the teachers are brought to an improbable meeting on the theme of 'school and popular music', at the end of which they will receive a record with a rare version of an Italian pop song; and a psychologist is always available to assist the teachers, rather than the students. The mottos of the schoolmaster are 'updating is everything' and 'the school must not form but inform'. The satirical intention is so strong that the Marilyn Monroe School looks like a carnivalesque image of a real school, a parody, a bizarre and preposterous place inhabited by laughable characters, like the always cheerful schoolmaster and the quasi-autistic secretary, Edo. In order to 'build' his school, Moretti seems to have taken to their extreme the main elements of the ultraliberal discourse on the school that dominated in the 1970s and early 1980s in Italy. The Italian scholastic system in those years had many faults and 'Italy lagged far behind other nations of similar standing … Secondary schooling was largely populated by a demoralised staff lacking incentives. Italy had one of the lowest staff/student ratios in secondary schooling Europe, but also the worst paid schoolteachers of any of the economically advanced nations' (Ginsborg 2001: 232). Within this discomforting panorama, attempts were made at opening up the school to the free-thinking and tolerant ideals carried by the revolution of 1968, an ultraliberal discourse made without addressing the serious faults and the structural gaps of the system. In particular, these attempts were often supported by the ideology that 'new' was synonymous with better.

It is worth retelling a joke told by Michele's father in *Ecce Bombo*: 'These are the results of a repressive education – think what you would have become if you had had a more modern education!' It is clear that, in *Bianca*, Professor Michele Apicella would favour a more traditional institution than the Marilyn Monroe School, but Moretti's discourse here is not against a progressive school model, rather against facile and generic choices, as well as against the idea that what is 'new' and 'trendy' is necessarily and automatically better than more traditional solutions. In an interview, Moretti listed the school in *Bianca* as an example of 'cultural vulgarity', together with the interviewer for Tele California in *Ecce Bombo* and the television competition in *Sogni d'oro*, and added that, when he satirises bad taste, he tries 'to have style in this mockery, to have more taste than the situations and the characters' which he criticises (quoted in Giovannini, Magrelli & Sesti 1986: 32).

In accordance with the opinion that Moretti principally criticises his own milieu, another object of his satire is the lure that popular culture exercises on intellectuals and on sophisticated people. Examples are the weakness of his characters for pop songs, which they like to sing out loud; for light but successful films, for instance Lean's *Doctor Zhivago* (*Palombella rossa*), or Lyne's *Flashdance* and Lattuada's *Anna* (*Dear Diary*); for famous actresses (Jennifer Beals and Silvana Mangano, both in *Dear Diary*); and for soap operas (*The Bold and the Beautiful*, once more in *Dear Diary*). Perhaps the most revealing episode is the one of *The Bold and the Beautiful* in which the intellectual Gerardo, a Joyce scholar, despite his rational scorn for television, which he has not watched even once in the last eleven years, finally and quickly succumbs to the fascination of soap operas and other popular entertainment programmes. When in Stromboli, Gerardo forces Nanni to ask a group of American tourists for information on the future episodes of the soap; when in Alicudi, the island without electricity, Gerardo writes a letter to the Pope, whom he berates for having excommunicated soap operas, and finally runs away from the secluded island shouting that Enzensberger and Popper are wrong, and that television is good for people. In this episode, as well as in all the others listed above, satire is quite mild and not caustic, as if Moretti looked with some sympathy at the power of popular culture and its fascination for educated people. The general tone is ironical rather than satirical, and in fact we will discuss these episodes again in the next section, devoted to irony. Perhaps the weakening of the corrosive attitude of Moretti's humour is not just due to the object of the satire but also to a more general turn in the film-maker's mind-set that manifests itself with *Dear Diary*. A critic has put forward the idea that it was perhaps the experience of cancer that changed Moretti, both on-screen and in real life, making him more relaxed and less aggressive. Asked about it in an interview, Moretti said that this might be true and that, after the stressful experience of his medical treatment, 'I felt reassured and reinvigorated, full of curiosity and desire to look around' (Comuzio 1993: 62). As another critic has noted, 'It is as if [in *Dear Diary*] irony had prevailed over fury, as if Nanni Moretti had decided that it will be a laugh (maybe the one of Michele as a child at the end of *Palombella rossa*?) that will triumph over all these awful things' (Martini 1993: 59).

We argue that irony was always a component of Moretti's comedy, and that Moretti was and is a true ironist. On the other hand, we agree that the balance between irony and satire varies across different films – for instance, in *Dear Diary* irony is prevalent over fury. In the next section, we will discuss Moretti's use of irony, intended as an attitude towards life.

Existential irony

As testified by the long history of the use of this term, the definition of irony is problematic.

> Its forms and functions are so diverse as to seem scarcely amenable to a single definition: Anglo-Saxon understatement, eighteenth-century raillery, Romantic Irony and schoolboy sarcasm are all forms of irony; Sophocles and Chaucer, Shakespeare and Kafka, Swift and Thomas Mann are all ironists; for Socrates irony was a standpoint, the governing principle of his intellectual activity; to Quintillian irony was a figure in rhetoric; to Karl Solger irony was the very principle of art; and to Cleanth Brooks irony is, 'the most general term we have for the kind of qualification which the various elements in a context receive from the context'. (Muecke 1980: 3)

Furthermore, it can be very difficult to distinguish between irony and satire, and between irony and other forms of the comic:

> The concept of irony is also obscured by the frequent and close conjunction of irony with satire and with such phenomena as the comic, the grotesque, the humorous, and the absurd ... But irony is not essentially related to satire, and when it is related in practice it is a relationship of means to end; and although irony is frequently found overlapping with the absurd or the comic it may also be found overlapping with the tragic. (Muecke 1980: 5)

Whereas irony can be and often is mixed with satire, the two are substantially different: satire, as we have seen above, is an attack on people, institutions or ideas motivated by deep discontent, anger, sometimes even hatred. Irony can be used as the channel for a satirical attack, but it is not per se characterised by the same feelings.

The most literal meaning of the term irony is that of succeeding in conveying the opposite of the literal sense of a phrase: 'the art of irony is that of saying something without really saying it' (Muecke 1980: 5). In this sense, Moretti is a true ironist: we seldom know for sure when he is joking and when he is serious, and it is often his facial expression that betrays the ironic meaning of his words. One straightforward example of this ironic speech can be found in *Aprile*: when a French journalist points out that it is inadmissible that a Fascist party form part of the government, as was the case in Italy at the time, Nanni begins to reply very seriously by repeating the official discourse, that the party has undergone revision and has distanced itself from past beliefs – at some point, though, he cannot refrain from laughing at what he is saying.

Rather than drawing the line at this generic sense of irony, as manifested in ironic statements and situations, we wish to adopt a more general view of irony that, in our opinion, better serves a study of Moretti's cinema. The definition that we find most useful is that of a detachment from life that can also be described as casting a dispassionate look upon it.[3] We will call this position existential irony, borrowing the expression from an essay by Andrew Cross on the concept of irony in Sören Kierkegaard (1988). We adopt and explore Kierkegaard's conception of irony in the knowledge that this has much in common with postmodern irony as subsequently formulated by philosophers such as Richard Rorty. In the next chapter, devoted to politics in Moretti's films, we will elucidate the postmodern aspect of Moretti's irony, and describe him as a 'liberal ironist' – someone who combines commitment with a sense of the contingency of his own commitment (Rorty 1989: 61). Here, we choose instead to refer to Kierkegaard, because his conceptualisation – as expounded in his university thesis, *The Concept of Irony with Continual Reference to Socrates* (1992a), as well as in his later *Concluding Unscientific Postscript* (1992b) – is useful in explaining the progression in Moretti's cinema from a 'negative' form of irony to a more 'positive' one.

In his essay, Cross regards Kierkegaard as a philosopher who considers irony as an attitude to life, rather than an act of speech.[4] This attitude is characterised by a detachment from life by which the ironist sees everything as a game. While engaging in social practices the ironist 'is merely playing at participating in them, without seeing himself as actually engaged in them … To invoke the metaphor Kierkegaard uses repeatedly, the ironist has risen above all society, all interpersonal interactions and relationships' (Cross 1988: 133–4). This position involves a feeling of superiority: 'Inwardly, for him, all of these aims, those goods, this society and its members are beneath him, beneath being taken seriously' (1988: 134).

It is precisely irony that is seen as the root of that feeling of superiority of which many critics and spectators alike accuse Moretti. The resentment towards the film-maker in the Italian audience and critics is as strong as the devotion for him, and in the assessment of Moretti's work it is easy to trace a line of aversion for Moretti's supposed arrogance and condescension, as in the following examples:

> The rather pretentious young film-maker says that he does not want to be a generational symbol and that he has nothing to prove, which is not very credible given that every sequence of his film … intends to mock a certain type of culture, certain ideological and aesthetical norms and certain types from the world of cinema and television. (Vergerio 1990: 156)

> When one is like Nanni Moretti – devoid of divine artistic inspiration – he should at least have the humility of being an apprentice, of learning, of being an artisan, as many other directors have … and instead it is precisely this humility that Moretti lacks. (Fini 1990: 165)

What these critics failed to see is that 'the ironist not only separates or dissociates himself from "the other[s]" but in a very real sense dissociates himself from himself' (Cross 1988: 135). We return here to our earlier considerations on the schizophrenic nature of Moretti's position as both film-maker and protagonist, subject of the observation and observed object, ironist and target of the ironist's derision. Of course other film-makers have done as Moretti has, and in particular Woody Allen. Yet while not being unique in the world of film-making, Moretti's comedy is nevertheless utterly original. Woody Allen, in fact, also criticises and mocks himself for being neurotic, insecure and infantile, but Moretti's self-irony has a much more radical character. As a critic has correctly judged when discussing *Bianca*, while Woody Allen trivialises neurosis, Moretti instead exacerbates it, takes it to a truly 'clinical' level (Philippon 1986: 50). Moretti's schizophrenic dissociation from himself is much more serious and painful than Allen's, at least in his darker films. Consequently, in order to study irony in Moretti's work, it is useful to separate the earlier films from *Dear Diary*, *Aprile* and *The Son's Room*. Whereas in the previous films the tone of Moretti's irony is prevalently dark and negative, in the later films it is lighter and more positive, and thus, we argue, more postmodern – the postmodern ironist, in fact, being convinced of the contingency of everything, does not perceive himself as being above the world, and never takes himself too seriously. As we have already suggested, Kierkegaard's thought is helpful in understanding and differentiating these two types of irony.

As suggested by Kierkegaard in *The Concept of Irony*, by dissociating himself from himself the ironist ceases to live a life of immediacy, 'a life whose content is determined by his given desires and ideals, by the norms of his society, without considering, in abstract reflection, whether his conception of the good has any genuine merit, whether his desires and ideals should be transformed or modified, whether his society's norms have any genuine authority over him' (Cross 1988: 137). Thus irony is for Kierkegaard the 'awakening of subjectivity'. In his earlier accounts of irony, though, as Cross shows, Kierkegaard's conception of irony is linked to negativity, in that the detachment from immediacy involves no positive conception of an alternative, more acceptable form of existence: 'as Kierkegaard repeatedly says, the ironist's freedom is merely "negative": it is a freedom from the constraint of immediacy, but not the positive freedom that would consist in realising a life that is genuinely his own' (1988: 138).

> For the ironic subject, the given actuality has lost its validity entirely; it has become for him an imperfect form that is a hindrance everywhere. But on the other hand, he does not possess the new. He knows only that the present does not match his idea ... he is continually pointing to something impending, but what it is he does not know. (Kierkegaard quoted in Cross 1998: 138)

Not only has the ironist – in this earlier conception – a nihilistic attitude towards social existence; negativity seems also to invest his conception of himself, because his position as ironist is unachievable. In fact, either he regards himself as different from and superior to others, but then his irony is not comprehensive (in that he does not exercise irony on his own irony); or he does mock himself, 'in which case he can no longer regard himself as different from the others and is once again not an ironist' (1988: 139).

Moretti's first films seem to us to be dominated by a dark, negative irony, which can well be described by Kierkegaard's concept of 'infinite absolute negativity'. We believe that the split between Moretti as an ironist and his persona as target of the irony is more dramatic in his work before *Dear Diary*. In the early films Moretti paints himself as painfully weak, fragile, neurotic and incompetent, when not as totally mad. In *Io sono un autarchico*, for instance, Michele is portrayed as weaker than his wife, more childish than his child, unsure of what he wants to do, and unconvinced of what he is doing. His humour is corrosive and life is painted as an absurdity – as becomes clear in the paradoxical scenes of the training camp for the actors, who even are at one stage attacked by Indians. His character presents similar characteristics in *Ecce Bombo*: again in this film Michele is unable to relate to women, insecure of his masculinity, aggressive with his parents and his girlfriend, uncommitted to his male friends. Life is once again painted as utterly painful and absurd – examples of this negative feeling are the scene in which the group of friends wait all night long for the sun to rise, but miss it; the ending of the film, with all the friends setting off to see Olga but getting lost during the trip; or even the scene that gives the film its title, with the man on his bike shouting his absurd slogan, 'Ecce Bombo!'

In these three films, Moretti's attitude towards his protagonist is twofold: on the one hand he detaches himself from him, feels superior to him and can therefore mock him; on the other hand he knows that he is laughing at himself as well as at the absurdity of life, from which he sees no escape. The schizophrenia inherent in this process of detachment from oneself looms large in these first films, and materialises in the figure of the schizophrenic Olga. In subsequent films, this schizophrenia becomes even more pointed. In *Sogni d'oro* Moretti laughs at himself as a young film-maker who is convinced of his superiority, of being the only good new director in Italy, but one who is at the same time acutely insecure, dependent on his mother, envious of his rival, neurotic on the set, afraid of public debates and interviews. He is also painted as a bad son and a bad lover, incapable of showing interest in and affection for his mother and for the woman with whom he is in love. In *Bianca* Moretti's ironic gaze on himself reaches dramatic levels – an incompetent teacher, who is neither interested in his students nor in his subject; an impotent lover, who is unable to accept the affection of the woman of his dreams; and an obsessive freak who ends up murdering his friends. This abrasive self-irony continues with *La messa è finita*, in which Don Giulio fails as a priest, as a brother, as a son and as a friend: all his attempts at helping the people around him fail miserably. In *Palombella rossa* Moretti turns his irony on himself as a politician (he loses his memory and his beliefs vacillate) and also as a sportsman (he misses the penalty that would have given his team victory in the league). In these films, life is seen as painful; as we have explored in our second chapter, Moretti describes childhood ambiguously as a lost paradise and as a time of pain and unhappiness, but primarily as a phase of yearning for a fusion with the mother that, being unattainable, leaves the individual feeling incomplete and unhappy forever. Moretti does not seem able to point to a way out: Michele in *Bianca* has only the negative choice between never being loved or suffering in love; Don Giulio's family, friends and parishioners cannot be helped in any way; and the Communist MP in *Palombella rossa* exclaims after the match: 'I didn't expect more from the match, but from life!'

Palombella rossa is in fact a 'liminal' film, between the dark and negative irony of the first part of Moretti's career and the lighter and more positive irony of his most recent work. In this film, in fact, the mood seems to lift slightly, as if Moretti was beginning to discover that 'way out' which will transform his irony. In *Palombella rossa*, as we will argue in the final chapter, Moretti points in fact to the necessity of finding new ways of looking at and of describing ourselves, which will lead to a new (and better) life and society. Thus, despite the general negativity of Michele's situation in this film (a film which opens and closes with two car crashes), a positive solution is beginning to form in the character's mind. Whereas Don Giulio in the previous film found no better answer than that of retreating to Patagonia, an almost sub-human place, in *Palombella rossa* the idea that things can be improved here and now is beginning to emerge.

In his later work, *Concluding Unscientific Postscript*, Kierkegaard put forward the idea that the positive conception of an alternative mode of existence for oneself and for others allows the ironist to transcend the impasse previously described, and thus transcend his 'negative irony'.

[W]here there is life there is contradiction ... The tragic and the comic are the same inasmuch as both are contradiction, but *the tragic is suffering contradiction, and the comic is painless contradiction* … The comic interpretation produces the contradiction or allows it to become apparent by having *in mente* the way out; therefore the contradiction is painless. The tragic interpretation sees the contradiction and despairs over the way out. (Kierkegaard quoted in Cross 1988: 150)

We mentioned above how one critic argued that the experience of illness documented in *Dear Diary* allowed Moretti to see life with new eyes. We think that the process of maturing in Moretti (along with that of post-modernisation) was already at work and, as we have suggested, had began to manifest itself with *Palombella rossa*. It is nevertheless true that *Dear Diary* is the film in which self-discovery and maturity become fully patent, and with them a more cheerful and lighter irony. Moretti – this time as 'Nanni' – continues to be the target of the film-maker's irony but, one would say, in a less cynical way. In 'On My Vespa' Nanni is mocked for his looks – he is often shot from behind, looking up, wearing his helmet and with his arms behind his back, in a posture that reminds the spectator of the infant characters of the comic strip *Peanuts*; for his childish desire to be a good dancer; for his little manias, like that of crossing the Ponte Flaminio ('I don't know, I can't understand. I may be nuts, but I love this bridge. I need to cross it at least twice a day'); and for his penchant for popular culture icons, such as the film *Flashdance* and its protagonist, Jennifer Beals. Nanni paints himself as slightly 'off centre', as Jennifer Beals calls him: he often talks to people in the street, who predominantly look on him as a madman – an expedient that, on the one hand, allows Moretti to mock himself with an affability that was missing from his previous films and, on the other hand, shows Moretti's contradictory desires to be apart from society and, at the same time, to fit in it. One episode in particular seems to express this double movement of involvement in and detachment from the immediacy of life – Nanni is at a traffic light and an expensive convertible pulls up; he dismounts from his scooter and says to the car driver:

You know what I was thinking about? I was thinking about a very sad thing, that, even in a more decent society than this one, I will always be comfortable only with a minority of people. But not in the sense of those films in which there is a man and a woman who hate each other, who brawl with each other on a deserted island because the director does not believe in people. I believe in people, but not in the majority of people. I think I will always be comfortable and in agreement only with a minority. (*Dear Diary*)

Comedy here is produced by the reaction of the car driver, who is impassive throughout and as soon as the light turns green drives away saying, 'OK, good for you!' – but the irony resides in the fact that this rather bitter declaration of dissent with and distance from the majority of people in society is shared with a perfect stranger, as to confirm that contact with the others is both avoided and sought.

In 'Islands', Nanni mainly teases himself for his inability to concentrate and work, as well as for his little manias, like the compulsion to collect hundreds of newspaper articles over the years, which he later finds rather useless or even daunting, and once again his interest in popular culture (the Silvana Mangano film seen on TV). Nevertheless, irony in this episode focuses more on others, like Gerardo, whose initial revulsion for television suddenly turns into total dependence, or like the parents of the island of Salina, whose life is dominated by their children. Such episodes constitute examples of Moretti's traditional criticism of his own milieu – Gerardo is nothing other than an intellectual like Moretti, and we have highlighted how the film-maker himself is not free of the influence of popular culture; the parents of Salina, who had a child when they were over thirty or forty and then looked after him or her almost obsessively, are not very different from the director himself, whom we will see dealing with his only child in *Aprile*.

In the last episode satire re-emerges strongly and its target, as we have already discussed, is the entire category of doctors. Irony, instead, concentrates once more on Nanni, and is perhaps used to lighten the impact of the subject matter – the cancer experienced by Moretti in real life. The (affable) ironic gaze of the director concentrates on his own persona, we would even say on his own body, as if to highlight the fragility and awkwardness of the human condition, as when we see him immersed in an absurd bath full of oat flakes, which are supposed to lessen the itch, or sitting between two Chinese doctors who take his pulse, or walking on a beach wearing his cotton socks and long-sleeved shirt, as prescribed by a dermatologist. In other words, Moretti in 'Doctors' depicts himself as frail and impotent: after a visit in which a consultant has suggested that his itch is psychological, Nanni moans in pure Woody Allen style: 'And if it is down to me, I am not going to make it!'

Even if this self-critical attitude is also present in the previous films, in *Dear Diary* the irony is less caustic and the general mood of the film is jubilant, despite the dark theme of 'Doctors' or the episode of the site of Pasolini's murder in 'On My Vespa'. Nanni is self-indulgent, happier with life, more understanding with other people. This does not mean that his habitual critical attitude towards the homogenised capitalist society has disappeared: contemporary Italian films and film criticism; American horror movies; the property market; the shameful 'monument' in memory of Pasolini; the incommunicability between the various 'islands' in Italian society; and the arrogance and ignorance of doctors, all become targets of his satire.

In *Aprile* Nanni mocks himself for being hopeless as a citizen and as a politician, since he never sent any of the many letters of protest that he wrote in his life; when he finally takes to the podium to give a speech, he does so at Hyde Park Corner in London, as if he were improvising as a preacher. He is also hopeless as a husband and a father, since he seems unable to support and give strength to his partner, and after the birth of his child he is full of anxiety and doubt (when Nanni and Silvia give their child his first bath, for instance, he contrasts the 'firm grip' of the mother with the 'insecure grip' of the father); finally, he is also portrayed as an inept film-maker, who is unable to make neither a documentary on Italy nor a musical on a Trotskyite pastry cook in 1950s Italy. Nanni also displays some of his customary manias, like keeping newspaper articles for years, or attaching much importance to the 'right' shoes (in this case they are those of the yet unborn Pietro). Nanni accuses himself of a lack of courage throughout the film but – as in *Dear Diary* – the tone of his irony is clearly more cheerful than in the earlier films. Despite the self-criticism, Nanni has found a 'way out' and is no longer so negative about life: Pietro is beautiful and Nanni as a father might be unconfident, but is also very caring and affectionate; his cinema work is always a painful experience, but in the end Nanni makes both the documentary and the musical; and life might be short, as the measuring tape of his friend shows him, but Nanni has understood that it is absurd to force himself to do things that he finds daunting and depressing, and that he should rather do the things he likes. As suggested in chapter two, paternity seems to be a truly positive experience which helps the film-maker (and his character) to lighten up and to see life in a different manner.

It seems difficult to talk about irony in the context of such a sorrowful film as *The Son's Room*; nevertheless, we suggest that Moretti's new attitude to life, his having identified a 'way out', has by no means been reversed in this film. Giovanni is not the dissociated, schizophrenic character that Michele was. Interestingly, the old Michele's extreme behaviour patterns, his paranoia and craziness, are now 'carried' by Giovanni's patients, who represent all that Moretti's character has overcome and left behind. In the first half of the film Giovanni is, instead, balanced, contented, passionately in love with his wife, at ease in his role of father and affectionate and attentive towards his children. Nevertheless, we do not see Giovanni as a 'new' character for Moretti (as have many critics), or even as the first 'real' and non-autobiographical protagonist that the film-maker has created. Giovanni, in fact, is best seen as the mature and more successful version of the old character, with his dream of the perfect family in which the parents love one another deeply and the relationship with the children is warm and well-balanced; but also with his wish to have an active, leading role in the community through which he has the opportunity to help others;[5] with his constitutive insecurity, which is here less acute and pathological, but which nevertheless manifests itself both before and, more dramatically, after the tragedy; with his humour and self-irony; and with his little manias (the glass of water he drinks in the opening sequence, which 'comes'

Giovanni (Nanni Moretti) jogging with his son in *The Son's Room* (2001)

from *Dear Diary*; the passion of singing Italian popular songs aloud; the interest in active sport). The impression is one of continuity as well as of improvement.

We argue that *The Son's Room* comes 'naturally' after the much more cheerful *Dear Diary* and *Aprile*. In his process of growth and development, as we have discussed, Moretti has discovered a 'way out', has become able to see that a better form of existence is possible. This does not mean that he loses the ability to see the contradictions of life, but that he gains the ability to see them without so much suffering, as Kierkegaard asserted. It is as if with this film Moretti wanted to remind himself – and us – that a positive attitude does not mean that the contradictory and the tragic have been removed from life. Although the unspeakable grief barely eases in the last sequences, we are left with the impression that Giovanni's life is still both worth living and possible to live. The morning after their night-time journey towards France, Giovanni and his wife Paola share the perception that life might become bearable again, that there might be a 'way out'; significantly, this perception materialises in their common laughter – they become able again to see the irony of the situation, the irony of life.

Conclusion

Alongside the evolution of his conception of the family and of the relationship of the individual to this ancient institution, as expounded in the previous chapter of this book, Moretti's more general philosophical stance also evolved with the years. While having always been an ironist, his growth and evolution transformed his irony from a 'negative' irony that does not 'possess the new', in Kierkegaard's words, to a more positive ironic position, which is able to 'see a way out' and to imagine better forms of existence. Although this evolution is apparently responsible for a mellowing of Moretti's critical stance, satire not only is always present in his films, but – as *Dear Diary* and *Aprile* testify – in a sense has become even more effective, because it is supported by a more focused vision of life and of the ways how our experience of our existence here and now may be improved. Not surprisingly, it was after conquering this new vision and after making the diary films that real-life Moretti also became more active and incisive in his political activism, as we will discuss in the next and concluding chapter devoted to politics.

CHAPTER FOUR

Say Something Left-wing! The Language of Postmodern Politics

An historical act can only be performed by 'collective man', and this presupposes the attainment of a 'cultural-social' unity through which a multiplicity of dispersed wills, with heterogeneous aims, are welded together with a single aim, on the basis of an equal and common conception of the world, operating in transitory bursts (in emotional ways) or permanently (where the intellectual base is so well rooted, assimilated and experienced that it becomes passion). Since this is the way things happen, great importance is assumed by the general question of language, that is, the question of collectively attaining a single cultural 'climate'.

– Antonio Gramsci (1992: 349)

Politics in postmodernity is recognised to be constructed in language; politics *is* language.

– John R. Gibbins & Bo Reimer (1999: 113)

D'Alema, react, say something, react, say something, answer, say something left-wing, say something even not left-wing, something civilised!

    – Nanni Moretti, *Aprile*

It is obvious that Moretti's is a political cinema. His only films in which politics is not overtly discussed are, to date, *Bianca* and *The Son's Room*. Practically all of his filmic incarnations make openly political (and polemical) comments, and many of them are or have been politically active. Televised images of real-life Italian politicians and political events are shown and commented on in *Aprile*; the documentary *La cosa* is made up of filmed debates between grassroots members of PCI on the change of name of the party proposed by its then leader Achille Occhetto after the fall of the Berlin Wall in 1989. In *L'unico paese al mondo 9*, a section of a collective film that he also produced, Moretti denounces as anomalous the candidature of Silvio Berlusconi, owner of a media empire, in the general election of 1994. Moretti also engaged in active politics in his youth, taking part in extra-parliamentary groups; recently, he has taken a public position against the second Berlusconi government and has become, perhaps unintentionally, a recognised leader of the popular movement of dissent against it. The way in which this new phase of political activism has begun has interesting points of contact with the way in which Moretti presents himself as a politician on screen.

A humble successful politician

On Saturday 2 February 2002, at the end of a political rally in Piazza Navona, Rome, Moretti unexpectedly took the podium and accused the leaders of Ulivo (the centre-left coalition), who had just delivered their speeches, of being bureaucrats incapable of self-criticism and of talking 'to the head, the heart and soul of the people'. He praised the speech of Professor Pardi, almost a newcomer, and defined him 'the new leader of Ulivo', and accused the left of underestimating the impact of Emilio Fede, a Berlusconi-supporter and head of the news for one of Berlusconi's television channels, ReteQuattro. He blamed Berlusconi for winning votes through his television channels, and Ulivo for allowing him to win the election with a timid political campaign.

One of the two political leaders directly accused by the film-maker, Francesco Rutelli (former Mayor of Rome, current leader of Ulivo and losing challenger to Berlusconi in the 2001 general election), defined Moretti's speech as 'an artist's cry', and commented: 'It is always useful that an intellectual talks and says what he thinks. Obviously it cannot be taken for granted that an intellectual is also a good politician, and it is not compulsory to follow him' (Rosso 2002: 2). With this declaration, given immediately after Moretti's speech, Rutelli apparently attempted to lessen Moretti's criticism, suggesting that the film-maker is only an artist, an intellectual and, as such, his opinions are not as consequential as those of a professional politician. Several other public figures also pointed to the fact that Moretti is a man of cinema, in some cases with a disparaging intention, as is clear from the words of the former President of the Republic Francesco Cossiga, who defined Moretti as *un guitto che si è montato la testa* – a stroller-artist who has become big-headed ('Rutelli a Moretti: Polemiche distruttive', 2002).

Immediately after his short accusatory speech, Moretti himself declared to a journalist for the Italian newspaper *la Repubblica*: 'I am not a politician, I do not know how to do politics' (De Gregorio 2002: 3). In the same interview, Moretti referred instead to the leaders of Ulivo as 'professional politicians', but also advocated his own right, as an elector of those politicians, to criticise them. This attitude is fully consistent with the portrayal of himself that Moretti realises through his films, as a humble, unimportant, ordinary person, as opposed to an outstanding artist, an influential intellectual, or a successful politician.[1] Although politics always played an important role in his life and in his films, Moretti portrays himself as an impotent and failed politician particularly in *Aprile* and in *Palombella rossa*. In *Aprile* we are shown the numerous political letters that Moretti wrote in his life, but never sent to their addressees, such as communist youth organisations, a leftist weekly magazine, *L'Espresso*,[2] and the old Italian Communist Party (PCI). Eventually the film-maker takes these letters to Hyde Park Corner in London, a place where every Sunday various evangelists and eccentrics share their ideas with impromptu audiences. He throws the letters away when giving a speech about the models of Italian socialism. The very context in which Moretti's speech is delivered undermines the seriousness of the ideas discussed. Moreover, to add to the impression that his political discourse cannot be treated seriously, he juxtaposes it with the sermons of some typical

Hyde Park preachers, who utter absurdities about the imminent coming of Jesus and similar issues.

In *Palombella rossa* Moretti plays a Communist MP who, after giving a momentous speech on TV during the general election campaign, suffers a loss of memory. People keep coming up to him to congratulate him on the courage and audacity of his speech, of which he cannot remember one word. Intriguingly, after his real-life speech in Piazza Navona, Moretti confessed to a journalist that he could not remember anything of what he had just said and asked her to repeat his speech to him: 'Sorry, I am a bit agitated. I am not used to it, I don't even fully realise what has happened ... did I talk a lot? ... And what did I say exactly?' (De Gregorio 2002: 3). One even wonders whether Moretti truly suffered a loss of memory, or whether he staged it, as part of the constant game of reflections between his protagonist and his off-screen personas.

Despite Moretti's humility, and despite the suggestion that, as he is not a politician, his political opinions should not be taken seriously, the film-maker's public outcry triggered a great upheaval and an animated debate in the left, and dominated the front pages of most Italian daily newspapers for the three following days, as well as the news programmes of both the public and private broadcasting services. *La Repubblica* conducted a survey amongst the readers of its on-line version, asking them whether Moretti was 'right or wrong', and collected 95 per cent of replies in agreement with Moretti's opinion (Cf. 'Il sondaggio. Ulivo, il caso Moretti', 2002). A debate via email was opened and, according to *la Repubblica*, hundreds of messages were received (Caporale 2002). In the following months, Moretti continued to attract the attention of the media, by participating in public meetings and demonstrations against the government. The impact of Moretti's speech in Piazza Navona can be measured by the decision of a group of leaders of the DS (merger of the ex-Communist Party PDS with various left-wing forces that took shape in 1998), announced on 7 April 2002, to form a new branch within the coalition in order to bring together all the new democratic forces that emerged in Italian society after Moretti's speech. Significantly, this branch was called Aprile, after the title of Moretti's film.

Moretti's outcry, in other words, was a political speech, which had serious political consequences and also raised noteworthy agreement amongst the public who were present and among the wider electorate of the left. Regardless of the film-maker's frequent assertions, both in real life and in his films, of being a non-politician or a failed politician, with his speech Moretti did politics. Moreover, Moretti's cinematic discourse is, we suggest, incisively and radically political. In this chapter, we concentrate on his cinema rather than on his off-screen activism, and we will study his three most political films to date: *Palombella rossa*, *La cosa* and *Aprile*. Before doing so, it is useful to explain that we will consider 'politics' as a discourse and as an open field 'where forces and relations, in the economy, in society, in culture, have to be actively worked on to produce particular forms of power, forms of domination' (Hall 1988: 169). We will site our analysis within the crisis of party politics in general and of the left in particular that constitutes the framework within which Moretti's political discourse is inscribed.

Postmodern politics and the crisis of the left

As Stuart Hall has recalled, the revolutionary events of 1968 marked the beginning of a new era, in which being radical no longer simply meant identifying with radical party politics but, conversely, being 'radically against *all* parties, party lines and party bureaucracies' (Hall 1988: 181). In the last thirty years, a period that roughly equates with what in this chapter we will refer to as the postmodern era, politics in general (radical and moderate) was marked by a widespread loss of faith in parties and in traditional macropolitics, a feeling also associated with a loss of faith in the capability of democracy to solve social problems. In the post-ideological polity, politics has ceased to be governed by the great, all-encompassing visions that belonged to modernity. The crisis undergone by socialism in the last twenty years – a crisis that escalated during the 1980s and exploded at the end of the decade with the fall of the Berlin Wall and the dissolution of the Soviet Union – has deeply changed the political panorama of both Europe and the Western world at large. The most evident effects of this process (as well as of other processes such as the development of disorganised capitalism and the diffusion of the postmodern condition) are the crises of traditional, all-encompassing ideologies; the widespread loss of interest in conventional political discourse; the growth of micropolitics, that is of movements, small parties and coalitions founded on and devoted to single socio-political issues; the increased centrality of questions that were only tangential to modernist politics, such as gender, sexuality, ecology, and the quality of life; the rise of 'identity politics', with the result that 'group identity (rather than class interest) has become the chief medium of political mobilisation' (Good & Velody 1998: 8); an increased tension between the global and the local; and the return of an ethnic component in politics. Such a situation is widely deemed to be very unstable and unpredictable, both by those who judge it in a positive manner and by those who read it in negative or even apocalyptic terms. Against this backdrop of crisis of the old and of change, we wish to look at the specific crisis of left-wing politics.

In his *The Hard Road to Renewal: Thatcherism and the Crisis of the Left*, Hall put forward a number of explanations for the lack of effectiveness and success of the British Labour Party and of European left-wing parties in general from the mid-1970s onward. Although published in 1988, Hall's insights are, in our opinion, still valid today, and in fact his book continues to be widely read. Today, at the time of writing, New Labour is in government in Britain, though Tony Blair's politics are, according to many, largely right-wing (at least according to conventional and certainly fading criteria of distinction between the right and the left), while Italy has a centre-right government led by Silvio Berlusconi. More generally, Western left-wing parties, despite some sporadic local successes, are still far from recovering from the fall of Communism and are struggling to find new ways forward. One of these hypothesis of change is, for instance, sociologist Anthony Giddens' 'third way' between socialism and neo-liberalism (Giddens 1998), which inspired a series of conventions of Prime Ministers and Heads of State of the left that have been taking place since the late 1990s in Washington, Florence, Berlin, Stockholm and London. The fact that Giddens' ideas, which are criticised by many commentators for being too right-wing, are supported and implemented by Tony Blair in Britain seems to us to confirm the difficulty for the left of finding a way out of the crisis without betraying the project of socialism.

Hall adopts a Gramscian vision – which we espouse – of politics as 'production', as an open discourse whose outcome depends on the relationship between forces that are active at any particular moment. In this contingent conception, which Hall derives from his reading of Gramsci's *Prison Notebooks*, politics is not 'an arena which simply reflects already unified collective political identities, already constituted forms of struggle' (Hall 1988: 169), it is rather an open field, in which success depends on the ability to produce, to forge, to impose a certain discourse: 'Gramsci understands that politics is a much expanded field; that, especially in societies of our kind, the sites on which power is constituted will be enormously varied. We are living through the proliferation of the sites of power and antagonism in modern society' (1988: 168).

According to Hall's analysis, the problem of left-wing parties (at the end of the 1980s for Hall, and even today in our opinion) is their lack of a new historical project (which on the contrary the right has), as well as their failure to see the contradictory nature of human beings and of social identities, and to understand politics as production, rather than as a given.

> [The left] does not see that it is possible to connect with the ordinary feelings and experiences which people have in their everyday lives, and yet to articulate them progressively to a more advanced, modern form of social consciousness. It is not actively looking for and working upon the enormous diversity of social forces in our society. It does not see that it is in the very nature of modern capitalist civilisation to proliferate the centres of power, and thus to draw more and more areas of life into social antagonism. It does not recognise that the identities which people carry in their heads – their subjectivities, their cultural life, their sexual life, their family life and their ethnic identities, are always incomplete and have become massively politicised. (Hall 1988: 171)

European left-wing parties, including the Italian PDS (Democratic Party of the Left – the moderate component of the former PCI), are still dominated by a bureaucratic conception of politics and thus fail to see how the experience of micropolitics is today deepening the populace's participation in democratic life. Their suspicious attitude towards social movements and popular protests not instigated and organised by the parties themselves is a signal of the gap between the leaders and the people, a gap that was already castigated by Gramsci himself. This gap is deepened by a lack of understanding of the contingency of the political field, and of the importance of political speech for the establishment and strengthening of a political hegemony. As Hall admonishes, and as world events have taught us, socialism is not an inevitable outcome of history, and the 'socialist man' – intended as a compact and stable set of needs, desires and values – no longer exists, if he ever did. Political beliefs do not straightforwardly follow from one's belonging to a certain social class – particularly in a world in which the traditional criteria for class division are changing or even, as some would have it, disappearing. Thus, socialist ideas will prevail if the socialist discourse is convincing, if it offers new and useful ways of articulating needs, protests and frustrations.

Whereas the left at this historical conjuncture seems unable to understand the socio-economic and political field, the right has been and continues to be very successful at doing so. Hall's analysis of Thatcherism is a very useful paradigm for a critique of the Berlusconi phenomenon in Italy. The project of both leaders is in fact rooted in the rejection of the welfare state, on the presupposition that this has corrupted both the state and the people: 'Thatcherism's project was to transform the state in order to restructure society; to decentre, to displace the whole post-war formation; to reverse the political culture which had formed the basis of the political settlement – the historic compromise between labour and capital – which had been in place from 1945 onwards' (1988: 163). According to Hall, Thatcher transformed the people's thinking, their 'common sense', which had been constructed around the notion that the market would never again be used as sole criterion to measure the needs of society, and that the welfare state was here to stay. Thatcher dismantled that project and substituted it with something else, the uneven development of capitalist modernisation, and while doing so she replaced the word *equality* with the word *freedom*. According to Hall, Thatcher, and we would suggest Berlusconi too, have understood that 'you have to struggle to implant the notion of the market; and that, if you talk about it well enough, effectively and persuasively enough, you can touch people's understanding of how they live and work, and make a new kind of sense about what's wrong with society and what to do about it' (1988: 188). By doing so, they have gone deep 'into the heartland of traditional labour support: skilled workers; working women; young people' (ibid.).

The task was even easier for Berlusconi than it was for Thatcher. The first Berlusconi government (1994) came at the height of a long phase of widespread and deep popular disillusionment with party politics and 'particracy', a phase concluded by the judicial inquiry into political corruption that wiped away the parties that had dominated the scene for forty years: the Christian Democrats and the Socialists. During the general election campaign of March 1994, it was easy to demonstrate that the old parties were synonymous with particracy, and that the particracy was synonymous with corruption. In spite of the fact that he had flourished in that political system, Berlusconi described himself as 'politically innocent' and proposed his own economic success as a new paradigm of development for the country: 'Berlusconi's message of economic liberalism – tax cuts, privatisation, and a million new jobs in the medium term ... had an electrifying appeal, tapping the mood of many people who felt excluded from and alienated by the old political elite' (Bufacchi & Burgess 2001: 170). The conjugation of politics and market in contemporary Italy is embodied by Berlusconi's project to transform the country into a firm that must be fit to compete on the scene of global capitalism. The right has managed to impose its new vocabulary and has thus conquered hegemony, while the left is struggling to come out of old metaphors but has not yet been able to replace them with new, effective ones.

In this chapter, we will suggest that Moretti has identified the same topics here discussed as the reasons for the crisis of the left, and has incisively pointed to them in his films. In the course of his oeuvre he has constructed a character somewhere between fiction and autobiography who proudly declares his individuality and his distrust of party politics, but who also believes that socialism is still very much needed in Italy and in the world at large. In *Aprile* he accuses the leaders of the left of a lack of charisma and of an attachment to old-style bureaucracy. In *Palombella rossa* he calls for the opening up of the party to the people and for a total change in its purpose and structure. In *La cosa* he shows the discontent and frustration of the grassroots resulting from their disconnection from the party, and points to the growing socio-political discourses that the left should get hold of and organise in a new socialist programme: sustainable development, pacifism and participatory democracy. In *Aprile* he adds to these the liberal themes of antifascism, of the defence of free press and speech, as well as of the independence of the judiciary. Overall, he shows the importance of language in political struggle and offers new metaphorical redescriptions of the moderate left-wing community. Before conducting a critique of his political discourse, we pause to examine how a political discourse can be and has been articulated through the medium of film.

The discourse on/of political cinema: realism and authority

There are two viable contrasting approaches to considering the relationship between politics and cinema: according to the first, all films are necessarily and unavoidably political in that, intentionally or unintentionally, they either embrace or contradict a given vision of the world. The second position, in contrast, defines as political only a limited number of films that directly present and support a precise political stance and/or expose and condemn a certain ideology.

The first approach stems from the debate on cinema and ideology raised in the aftermath of the revolutionary events of 1968 by the French journals *Cinéthique* and *Cahiers du cinéma*, a debate which owed much to post-Marxist theorists such as Kracauer, Brecht, Benjamin, Lukàcs, Adorno, Horkeimer, Althusser and Foucault, and which continued in the following years, involving many contributions in different journals, including *La Nouvelle Critique*, *Screen* and *Afterimage*.[3] The idea that all films are political is spelled out in some of the most important contributions, and with extreme clarity in Jean-Louis Baudry's and in Jean-Louis Comolli's articles on the apparatus which uncover the ideological foundation of the functioning of the cinema as a machine for the production of meaning (cf. Baudry 1978; Comolli & Narboni 1976). The same perspective was also embraced with polemical vigour by feminist film theory, and served as a basis from which to deconstruct the functioning of patriarchal cinema (cf. Johnston 1973; Mulvey 1975).

The logical passage from this all-embracing approach to the second, more restricted methodology is summarised by Mike Wayne as follows: 'All films are political, but films are not all political in the same way' (Wayne 2001: 1). The practice of film criticism necessitates instruments to isolate and analyse a set of texts that are intentionally political. The question that arises, then, is in what different ways can films be political?

One of the ways in which the adjective 'political' has been used is to define and distinguish between two wide-ranging categories of films, those of overt propaganda and state support – both left-wing and right-wing, famous examples of which are, respectively, Soviet montage and Nazi cinema – and those of criticism and condemnation of the status quo, an example of which is Italian Neorealism. Whereas the films belonging to the first group are generally fully supported by a totalitarian state, the second category is at the opposition, and therefore often countered through censorship, negative press and lack of funding.

Very frequently, and also in the present day, the term 'political' has been specifically used as a synonym of 'Marxist' and 'revolutionary'. In his recent book on *Political Film*, for instance, Wayne proposes to include in this category only texts that 'address unequal access to and distribution of material and cultural resources, and the hierarchies of legitimacy and status accorded to those differentials' (2001: 1). The author identifies political cinema with Third Cinema, a cinema of social and cultural commitment and emancipation, and defines this in relation to and in contrast with the other two prevailing categories of films, First Cinema (dominant, mainstream) and Second Cinema (art, authorial). Expressions such as Third Cinema, revolutionary cinema, counter cinema, deconstructive film and guerrilla film-making emerged in the late 1960s and early 1970s, in parallel with the theoretical debate on film and ideology, and have been used by critics with reference to different cinematic practices, including experimental film-making, the avant-garde, women's cinema, Third World cinema, art-house cinema and even mainstream cinema.[4] In all cases, critics referred to a revolutionary filmic theory and practice which tended to deconstruct mainstream cinema both in aesthetic and political terms.

In Marxist terms, the most significant and thorny question which arises in any discussion on political cinema is that of realism, because of its conflicting abilities to convey a progressive ideological stance or at least to denounce a certain social condition (see Marx's praise of Balzac), and to create a narcotic dominant dramatic form (see Brecht's criticism of mass-produced culture). Obviously, the question of realism is problematic not only in terms of Marxist theory, but more in general as a philosophical issue. The Marxist view on realism in art has changed over the years – it suffices to remember how, in the post-revolutionary Soviet cinema of the 1920s, visual experimentalism was preferred over traditional, compromised forms of film-making (a position also embraced by such anti-bourgeois and Marx-influenced avant-garde movements such as Dada and Surrealism), whereas in the 1930s Stalin's dogma of socialist realism put an end to experimentation, while being yet another form of anti-realism. Realism as an instrument of resistance and social criticism gained particular importance through Italian Neorealism and, thanks to this movement's influence, in the post-war era Marxists 'favoured an aesthetic of progressive realism, which stood against the superficiality of entertainment and allowed for social criticism' (Kleinhans 1998: 108), and thus praised such auteurs as Luchino Visconti, Jean Renoir, Stanley Kubrick and Orson Welles.

Under the influence of Althusser and Foucault, the question of realism in film radically changed perspective. From a Western/white/male Marxist perspective, cinema is 'the product of the ideology of the economic system that produces it and sells it' (Comolli & Narboni 1976: 12) and, as a product of the capitalist economic system, bourgeois cinema is interested in 'hiding the productive work that is the origin of surplus value' (Leblanc quoted in Casetti 1999: 187). From a Third World perspective, cinema is imperialistic and so far 'films only dealt with effect, never with cause; it was cinema of the mystification or anti-historicism. It was *surplus value* cinema' (Solanas & Getino 1976: 44). For feminist theorists, both mainstream and art-house cinemas are the product of patriarchal society, and tend to place women outside history through their realism: 'The law of verisimilitude (that which determines the impression of realism) in the cinema is precisely responsible for the repression of the image of woman and the celebration of her non-existence' (Johnston 1976: 211).

Consequently, cinema was deemed to be revolutionary, both by First and Third World Marxists, as well as by feminist theorists, when it resisted the illusionary cinema of bourgeois/imperialist/patriarchal realism, when it made manifest its own processes of fabrication, when it was self-aware and meta-cinematic. This approach was not devoid of problems. As Kleinhans writes:

The biggest change came in a shift in the left's analysis of commercial entertainment cinema as Hollywood film was reinterpreted as fundamentally realist. Thus a normative realism, understood as identical with Hollywood's practice of illusionism, was seen as producing a coherent imaginary subject position ... In contrast, a self-reflexive modernism and avant-garde practices can be read as themselves producing a dispersal of meaning and deconstructing the subject position, thus calling into question both illusionism and the dominant ideology. As a result, some interpreted an extreme formalism as sufficient to establish a work as politically radical, irrespective of content ... The problems of this type of analysis derived from two false assumptions: that ideology directly reflects class identity, and that the film was the sole source of meaning. (Kleinhans 1998: 110–11)

In other words, the whole history of the theorising on counter cinema resulted in an unsatisfactory critical practice that, for instance, led to consider as anti-bourgeois such diverse authors as Jean-Luc Godard and Douglas Sirk. This flawed perspective was finally to be corrected in more recent times by contesting the identification of anti-realistic with avant-garde, and of avant-garde with progressive, as Teresa De Lauretis did in her analysis of Michael Snow's *Presents* (De Lauretis 1984); as well as by placing films within their stylistic and socio-economic contexts and by examining them 'as produced by an interaction between a text and a spectator who was not understood as an ahistorical "subject", but as a historical person with social attributes of gender, race, class, age, nationality and so on' (Kleinhans 1998: 111). Attention began to be placed on the fact that films are not made in an economic vacuum and that the position of cinema with respect to the dominant ideology is conditioned by its cost – a characteristic that distinguishes it from other arts. The possibility of expressing radical and oppositional views through film must be thus analysed with reference to both economic and technical contexts. The introduction of lightweight cameras in the late 1950s and of video in the 1990s, for instance, partly modified the director's constrained situation; in specific cases, authors of counter cinema also found alternative ways of producing and of distributing films in order to circumvent censorship. Films are the product of their time and society (as much, as Marx would say, as ideology is the product of its time and society), and the perception of their political quality, as well as of their realism, unavoidably changes. Film movements that in their time broke with established conventions and were deemed as revolutionary have today lost some (or all) of their power of impact and appear almost mainstream to contemporary viewers. A clear example is Neorealism – a movement that at the time was considered to be shockingly realistic and was censored by the Italian Christian Democrat government for being explicitly Communist and subversive, but today is perceived as generically left-wing and pervaded by Christian humanism. It is worth recalling Kristin Thompson's analysis of *Bicycle Thieves'* production of the impression of reality, which for the author is constructed through an alternation of narrative and stylistic conventions and infringements of the same, and through the use of a 'balanced, rational, humanist' ideology (Thompson 1998: 204). Indeed, we agree with the by now prevalent belief that 'realism is an effect created by the artwork through the use of conventional devices' (1998: 197), and we take on Thompson's argument that '[realism] has the ability to be radical and defamiliarising if the main artistic styles of the time are highly abstract and have become automatised ... Realisms, then, come and go in the same sorts of cycles that characterise the history of other styles. After a period of defamiliarisation, the traits originally perceived as realistic will become automatised by repetition, and other, less realistic traits will take their places. Eventually other devices will be justified in quite a different way as relating to reality, and a new sort of realism will appear, with its own defamiliarising abilities' (1998: 198–9).

The recognition that all representations are symbolic, and thus there are no realist representations as such, as well as the critical shift in focus from the text to the socio-economic and stylistic contexts and to reception was somehow anticipated in 1971 by a contribution of Jean Patrick Lebel. Convinced that the ideology of the film is not intrinsic, and that, therefore, breaking the impression of reality is not enough to be revolutionary, Lebel suggested that a film's ideological position depended on the way directors use their material, on their ability to exploit the medium, and on the reactions that they generate in the public, 'along with the possibility, therefore, of affecting the orientation and attitudes of public opinion, as well as the possibility of changing the social meaning of cinema itself' (Casetti 1999: 193). This suggestion seems very appropriate to introduce a second issue of paramount importance when discussing political cinema: authority. Since, as we have highlighted in this condensed history of Marxist criticism of film, the perception of what is realist and reactionary, as well as what is revolutionary and oppositional, changes over time, the question arises how a given view gains authority in a particular socio-economic, historical conjuncture, and/or for particular audiences. Political cinema (or perhaps simply 'the cinema') is not just about producing or, conversely, effacing an effect of reality – two alternative practices depending on the perception of realism as, respectively, a constructive and beneficial reflection of a given social reality, or an illusionary representation that silences difference and masks oppression. Political cinema is also about telling the truth, or, in a relativistic, poststructuralist perspective, is about constructing a discourse, either through realism or its effacement, which is believed to be truthful and correct, at least by part of the audience. This question is of course problematic: in times of postmodern scepticism towards authority, of acknowledgement of the lack of fixed, objective viewpoints from which to assess discourses, the double task of the left-wing political film is harder than ever – on the one hand it has to demolish authority, on the other, in order to do this in a credible way, it has to construct the conditions of its own authority.

Both the questions of realism and of authority are of great relevance to Moretti's cinema. His films mostly break with realism, intended as the current mainstream style of representation, and distance the spectator from the customary experience of identification with the characters and the fictional world constructed on screen not only by mainstream cinema, but also by much European art-house film. Nevertheless, though Moretti's political position is clearly left-wing and oppositional, his cinema is not traditionally Marxist, and it does not meet Wayne's criterion of being devoted to addressing unequal access to and distribution of material and cultural resources. Moretti's left-wing position is best described as moderate, postmodern and post-dogmatic. Rather than making a militant cinema in classical Marxist terms – something that is far from impossible in postmodern times, as the cinema of Ken Loach testifies – from his very first films Moretti has reflected on the crisis of modern politics and the passage to postmodern politics. We will claim that, while not offering clear-cut answers and dogmatic solutions, Moretti is attempting a re-description of a community in crisis – the Italian and, more generally, the Western European moderate left.

Moretti's cinema as counter cinema

Moretti's first films are parodies of the life, beliefs and anxieties of the left-wing middle-class youth in Rome. As a critic has recently written about *Io sono un autarchico*, 'Culturally and ideologically, Michele's ironic disenchantment with the ways things are struck a nerve with Italian audiences. A year before the protest movements of 1977 shook up Italian society, Moretti was already nailing the banality behind fashionable slogans and satirising his generation's self-involvement' (Young 2002a: 57–8). The criticism of the confused commitment of the youth of the Italian middle-class appears in the Super-8 short *La sconfitta*, in which the young protagonist, Luciano, is full of doubts regarding his militancy in the extra-parliamentary left; in *Io sono un autarchico*, with parody of radical experimental theatre; and in *Ecce Bombo*, where a group of confused male friends engages in self-analysis meetings, attends (deserted) rock festivals and visits a commune organised on Stalinist lines. The left-wing bourgeois Italian youth was already presented in these films as confused and in crisis – something that perhaps depended less on them than on ideological shortcomings of the political organisations they referred to.

Moretti's criticism of the Italian left concentrates on the political positions taken by the parties that compose it, on the language used by their leaders, but also on the choices of specific followers. For instance, Giulio, the priest in *La messa è finita*, in his youth took part in extra-parliamentary activities and contributed to a radical newspaper, but when he finds out that one of his old friends is in jail for terrorist activities he completely dissents with him – an attitude that is also reconfirmed by Moretti's role as producer and protagonist of Mimmo Calopresti's *La seconda volta* (1995), in which he plays a university lecturer who in the 1970s became the target of a terrorist group's bullet in Turin. When meeting his aggressor for the 'second time' twenty years later, he seeks explanations from her but still finds it impossible to understand her choices. Whereas in *La sconfitta* Moretti teased the absurd dream of the Italian left-wing youth of living the phase 'before the revolution', in *Bianca* he addresses the effects of the free-thinking politics of the 1970s on the Italian schools, one of which is depicted in this film as a farcically radical place in which teachers are given in-work counselling, and information is deemed more important than education. In *Palombella rossa*, as we will see more in depth below, Moretti addresses the crisis of the left-wing electorate when confronted with the inconsistency of the PCI and its inability to offer adequate responses to the changes in society during the 1980s. In *Aprile* the left is accused of not having charismatic leaders, sufficient strength and a valid programme to oppose media magnate Silvio Berlusconi's political ascent. The lack of an original programme is indicated as a persistent fault of the Italian left, as seen in the Hyde Park Corner episode, in which Nanni reads a letter that he wrote (but did not send) to the extra parliamentary left in the early 1970s, in which he accused Italian Communism of following the model of the Soviet Union first, and then of Maoist China, instead of looking for a different, original Italian route. Left-wing politicians in *Aprile* are also blamed for being disconnected from the people and for lacking human qualities, as they failed to come to Brindisi after the accidental sinking of a boat of refugees from Albania. The Brindisi episode, which for Nanni is 'a symptom of the political and human absence of the left', reminds us of Hall's critique of British Labour during the Thatcher era – according to the author, instead of providing solutions to social problems, such as the closure of mines, Labour leaders preferred to rid themselves of them by way of being absent or silent (Hall 1988: 196–210).

The accusations of the left are counterbalanced by Moretti's evident pride at belonging to the Italian moderate Communist tradition, as can be seen in various episodes, among which are Michele's statements in *Palombella rossa* that capitalism has not resolved its own contradictions, and that PCI has many ideas for the easing of people's suffering and unhappiness (even if Michele's desperate tone of voice shows his lack of faith in the Party's ability to execute them); or even the episode in *Dear Diary* in which Nanni distances himself from the characters of the fictitious Italian film who are self critical of their past political activism – 'You shouted horrible things, the things I shouted were right and today I am a splendid 40 year old!'. Furthermore, criticism of the right is, although more sparse, certainly more intense than that of the left. Particularly strong are Moretti's criticisms of Berlusconi, of the ex-Fascist party Alleanza Nazionale and of Umberto Bossi's dissident ambitions that can be found in *Dear Diary*, in Moretti's episode of the collective film *L'unico paese al mondo*, and in *Aprile*.

Given this strong polemical attitude, it is tempting to describe Moretti in terms of counter cinema. His beginnings, for instance, were polemical and outside the industry, as we have explored in the Introduction. Secondly, Moretti's films present many of the formal characteristics widely ascribed to counter cinema. With the exception of *The Son's Room* and, less so, of *La messa è finita*, which their author has defined as his 'most realistic' works to date (cf. Young 2002a: 60), Moretti's films break with the illusionary realism of both mainstream and art-house production. This break is achieved by means of a strong meta-cinematic attitude. Characters at times speak directly into the lens, commenting on films, the Italian cinematic industry, film-makers and film critics. One of the most surprising (and amusing) anti-realistic and meta-cinematic moments occurs in *Io sono un autarchico*, when Michele phones his father asking him for the 'usual check', and then tells a friend that this phone call will prevent spectators from wondering how Michele maintains himself and his apartment without a job.

Realism is also challenged and broken in other ways: for instance, through an uncommon use of the camera, which up to *La messa è finita* is almost fixed, with long shots and virtually no montage. Furthermore, the ontological status of the image (the question whether it belongs to reality or dream) is sometimes difficult to establish, as happens extensively in *Sogni d'oro*, as well as more sparingly in other films. Examples are the final sequence of *La messa è finita*, with the couples dancing in the church at the end of the last mass celebrated by Don Giulio in Rome; and that of *Palombella rossa*, in which Michele and his daughter emerge from a car accident and climb over a hill along with other characters (including Michele as a child), towards a paper pulp sun. Often, the moments of unrealism are linked to (or highlighted by) the use of Italian pop songs, because the source of the song seems to be extra-diegetic, but then the characters begin to sing or dance to the music, thus creating a dream-like atmosphere.

Unrealism is also constructed through a very unusual use of space. In many of Moretti's films the image has no objective referent; screen space seems to exist independently of the objective world. As a reviewer of *Ecce Bombo* has noticed, for instance, Moretti's 'is a film that uses wonderfully the off-screen space to indicate the end of the social for saturation and implosion: it is a film à la Baudrillard' (Fargier quoted in De Bernardinis 2001: 54). The image, in other words, does not refer to anything other than itself, as if the off-screen space, the social, no longer existed. An example of Moretti's unusual attitude towards on-screen and off-screen space occurs in *Sogni d'oro*, when a bar in which Michele is playing pinball is invaded by actors who are playing a scene of Gigio Cimino's musical, thus challenging the diegetic status of the bar. Similar effects are achieved throughout *Palombella rossa*: 'what is particularly modern in *Palombella rossa* is the idea that the other scenes are all there, available, interwoven around this swimming pool which alone represents the depth from which things of the past re-emerge' (Daney 1995: 184–5). Time as well as space is a category that Moretti uses in an unrealistic manner: 'time in Moretti is pure abstraction, because everything comes out of the head of the character, and everything returns to it' (Toubiana quoted in Villa 1999: 60). In *Palombella rossa*, for instance, 'it is not possible to trace a stringent temporal progression, the actions set around the swimming pool are consumed in a radical a-temporality, where every single moment becomes dilated, syncopated, and repeated' (Villa 1999: 60).

Finally, the effect of reality is broken by the strong impression that each of Moretti's films is not an independent work of fiction, but constitutes a chapter of a wider autobiographical discourse – an effect achieved by the reappearance of the same biographical details and personality traits in all the films' protagonists, and reinforced by analogies with Moretti's real-life persona. Also, the use of non-actors (some of whom play themselves in their roles of family members and friends of real-life Nanni) simultaneously strengthens the autobiographical effect and the impression of unrealism. Realism is also effaced by the fragmentary nature of the narrative, which becomes even an anti-narrative in the 'diary films', *Dear Diary* and *Aprile*.

In the light of the critique of the theorisation on counter cinema, which we illustrated in the previous section of this chapter, we do not wish to straightforwardly associate these stylistic qualities of Moretti's cinema with political progressiveness. As De Lauretis has shown, counter cinema can also be reactionary, so that the analysis of the political stance in Moretti's films must go beyond considerations on their anti-realism – not only because it can as easily be argued that they are realistic as that they are anti-realistic. For instance, both the autobiographical element and the many references to society and to real-life events and people can be seen as creating, as well as effacing, an effect of reality. Furthermore, in spite of the many similarities, it is necessary to distinguish Moretti's production from that of most of the authors whom he has more than once indicated as his mentors: Carmelo Bene, the Taviani brothers, Bellocchio, Pasolini, Ferreri, Bertolucci and the French *nouvelle vague*.[5] Moretti's cinema not only is anti-dogmatic, but also post-dogmatic, utterly and radically postmodern. Our investigation will therefore distance itself from the 'classical' analysis of counter cinema and its stylistic trappings, and will instead concentrate on the discourse of postmodern politics as conveyed by Moretti's films.

Moretti as a liberal ironist

We believe that Moretti is best described as a 'liberal ironist', an expression and conception that we borrow from Richard Rorty (1989) – liberal, because in his films he incessantly advocates the liberal cause, by attracting attention to the suffering of individuals in our society; ironist, because he constantly addresses and highlights the contingency of language, community and conscience. Rorty's theories are particularly useful when discussing Moretti's cinema because of their emphasis on language – and we will show how precisely language is presented by Moretti as being at the core of the problem of contemporary politics.

A liberal ironist is described by Rorty as a person who believes that we are nothing but one more among Nature's experiments, and that there is no standpoint outside the particular historically conditioned and temporary vocabulary we are presently using. Ironists are 'never quite able to take themselves seriously because [they are] always aware that the terms in which they describe themselves are subject to change' (Rorty 1989: 73–4). Liberals are 'people for whom (to use Judith Shklar's definition) "cruelty is the worst thing they do"' (1989: 74), who take 'the morally relevant definition of a person ... to be "something that can be humiliated"', and whose 'sense of human solidarity is based on a sense of common danger, not on a common possession or a shared power' (1989: 91). Liberal ironists combine 'commitment with a sense of the contingency of their own commitment' (1989: 61). They engage in a constant activity of redescription; but whereas ironist theorists 'want a way of seeing their past which is incommensurable with all the ways in which the past has described itself ... ironist novelists are content with mere difference. Private autonomy can be gained by redescribing one's past in a way which had not occurred to the past' (1989: 101).

Moretti's similarity with Rorty's liberal ironist is significant. Firstly, he appears to be convinced of the contingency of language, and thus of conscience and community. His stubborn, annoyed insistence that 'words are important' and his dread of commonplaces, unjustified use of foreign terms and corruptions of the language testifies to his understanding of the importance of language itself, and that to use certain words (a certain language game, as Wittgenstein would put it) implies that one thinks in a certain way, because there is no thought outside language. As Michele meaningfully exclaims in *Palombella rossa*: 'He who speaks badly, thinks badly, and lives badly.' Furthermore, this emphasis on language is political, because it attracts attention to the fact that language is a tool of power. By replacing some words with others in political discourse, or by redefining the meaning of words, it is possible to shape political reality, and also to gain hegemony. Conversely, by using clichés, outdated words and expressions, one can lose hegemony.

As a liberal ironist, Moretti does not believe in a fixed standpoint from which to assess the world, and that the truth is 'out there'. In political terms, this translates into his refusal to identify with the Communist doctrine and to take out party membership. Although he participated in the activities of extra-parliamentary groups in the 1970s, even then he did not supinely accept the party line, and did not embrace extreme positions – as is clear from his criticism of terrorism. More and more so in the course of the years, Moretti has come to identify with the mainstream, moderate left, but his position is utterly polemical and anti-dogmatic. Notwithstanding his criticism and lack of compliance, or perhaps because of this, Moretti has ended up being a most reliable supporter of the liberal cause with which a certain section of the left identifies:

> In these politically confused times, Moretti has remained an un-wavering, even maddeningly obstinate moral beacon for the Italian left in films that bring together his political convictions and personal outrage with a searingly honest crusade against personal suffering, loneliness, and the impossibility of communicating through clichés. (Young 2002a: 61)

As this critic rightly suggested, in his films Moretti reveals his outrage for the suffering of the individual, caused by the cruelty of others (it is enough to pick out, from the many such examples, Don Giulio's mother in *La messa è finita*, who commits suicide after her husband left her for a much younger woman), as well as his sense of human solidarity as based on 'a sense of common danger' (as in the sudden loss of a child in *The Son's Room*). The fact that Moretti often plays unpleasant characters, who are aggressive, cruel and disrespectful of the feelings of others, confirms that he prefers to criticise in himself what he also disapproves of in others, that he does not put himself on a pulpit and dispense a truth inaccessible to others.

Moretti's progressive creation of an autobiographic opus testifies to his constant activity of redescription of himself and of the people (family, friends, people he met in his life, members of his community) who in their turn described him, a characteristic he shares with Rorty's ironist novelist. This activity of redescription results in self-creation, which is also the creation of a new cinematic language, a concept that an Italian critic has synthesised as follows: 'Nanni Moretti is the heir to Federico Fellini ... the only one able to reinvent, the only director in the world who makes cinema without cinema, who is totally self-sufficient, who proposes himself as *original* and who, precisely for these reasons, must necessarily and immodestly be (remain) author of himself' (Fittante 1998: 4). As we have already claimed in the course of this book, the frequent accusations of immodesty are counterbalanced by the opposite consideration, that Moretti's choice of autobiography, of being the 'author of himself', testifies to his self-irony, as these quotes suggest: 'From the beginning, I treated myself and my world not only with affection, but also with irony and distance. I made fun of myself, my generation, and the audience, something the left would never do' (quoted in Young 2002a: 51); 'Autobiography, if this is how we want to call it, interests me as cruelty towards myself' (quoted in Martini 1989: 66).

A further aspect that characterises Moretti as a liberal ironist is his attitude towards authority, which we have identified as one of the thorniest issues that left-wing political cinema must confront, particularly in postmodern times. Moretti's films dismantle authority by redescribing it in ironical terms; but the problem for the liberal ironist (and for the postmodern political film-maker) is, to borrow Rorty's words, 'how to debunk the ambitions of the powerful without sharing them' (1989: 103). In his discussion of Proust – an author whose work coincides with autobiographical redescription – Rorty maintains that the writer was able to 'rid himself of the fear that there was an antecedent truth about himself, a real essence which others might have detected', and that he 'was able to do so without claiming to know a truth which was hidden from the authority figures of his earlier years' (ibid.). Moretti's constant effort to redescribe himself, as opposed to congealing his own portrait, results in a similar denial of knowing a truth about himself. Furthermore, by undermining himself as a successful politician, an outstanding intellectual and an important film-maker, thus by denying to know a truth hidden from others, Moretti debunks authority without sharing it. We will see in the next section how Moretti articulates this discourse in his three most overtly political films. Before doing so, it is necessary to attract attention to the fact that, as Proust 'had become as much of an authority on the people whom he knew as his younger self had feared they might be an authority on him' (Rorty 1989: 102), Moretti has also become, perhaps unwillingly, a figure of authority in the panorama of Italian cinema, as well as an intellectual whose opinions are sought by the media. Moretti's visibility in Italian society is usually ascribed to the provocative quality of his films, to the unambiguous opinions he expresses on-screen on films, people and events, opinions that call the spectator to make an equally clear choice – either with Moretti, or against him. We believe that his ability to raise debate is rather due to the modernity of his cinema, as well as to the incisiveness of his political discourse. Moretti's films produce new metaphors – new vocabularies to talk about our society – both in terms of cinematic language and of speech at large.

We must invent a new language: Palombella rossa, La cosa and Aprile

Whereas in other films by Moretti politics as a subject matter surfaces intermittently in the narrative, in *Palombella rossa*, *La cosa* and *Aprile* it gains special relevance and takes centre stage – although in *Aprile* the private experience of paternity receives equal attention. The first two films discuss the crisis of the Italian Communist Party following the fall of Communism in the Eastern European bloc, one using fiction (if this can be called fiction) and one using documentary. *Aprile*, adopting the form of the diary, looks at two general elections in Italy (the first in 1994 won by the centre-right coalition led by media tycoon Silvio Berlusconi, the second in 1996 won by the centre-left coalition, Ulivo) as well as at other events, such as Umberto Bossi's declaration of independence of the northern region self-baptised as Padania (1996), and the landing of a boat full of Albanian refugees in Brindisi, Puglia (Spring 1997). In *Aprile* the PCI has disappeared and has been replaced by two parties, the moderate Democratic Party of the Left (PDS) and the radical Rifondazione Comunista.

In *Palombella rossa* and in *Aprile* Moretti – first as Michele Apicella, then as himself (or as Nanni, as we will call him in order to distinguish the film-maker from his filmic alter ego[6]) – tests himself with active politics; in *La cosa* he films active politics done by ordinary members of the party. We will argue that in each of these films doing politics in post-ideological Italy is seen as a process of inventing a new vocabulary, which is an activity of redescription, and a notion akin to Gramsci's 'fundamentally contingent, fundamentally open-ended' conception of politics as production (Hall 1998: 169).

Because Moretti is an ironist film-maker, this activity of redescription does not only affect the ideological field, but also the artistic sphere – thus, while he suggests that we search for a new political language, Moretti invents a new cinematic language. The two are deeply connected, as is clear from the following passage from an interview with Moretti about *Palombella rossa*: 'It is in the water that I want to say all these things [about Communism and capitalism], tiring myself out, to show the difficulty of starting from zero and the necessity to make cinema in a different manner, outside the established canons and practice' (Moretti quoted in De Bernardinis 2001: 8). Furthermore, in *Palombella rossa* and *Aprile*, by redescribing himself with pitiless self-irony, Moretti represents himself as a failed politician and as a not-outstanding intellectual, thereby denying that he knows a truth hidden from the figures of authority he criticises. In this manner, Moretti debunks authority without sharing it; nevertheless, we will argue that, by inventing a new cinematic language, Moretti himself paradoxically becomes an authority. Finally, by historicising Italian Communism, Moretti shows to be a liberal ironist, convinced of the contingency of language and community.

Palombella rossa was released in 1989, a year which was the apex of a long difficult phase for Italian as well as European Communism. 'The 1980s proved a very difficult decade for the [Communist Party], as it did for the European left as a whole. The rapid changes that were taking place in society were undermining the left's traditional electorate and bringing into question many of its old ideological certainties' (Ginsborg 2001: 157). In 1982, after the imposition of martial law in Poland, the leader of PCI, Enrico Berlinguer, publicly criticised the Soviet model of socialism, a break that for many came too late, but that placed PCI at the vanguard of Western European Communist parties. Unfortunately, although 'Berlinguer believed passionately that the Italian Communists were different … this difference was not translated into a convincing programme of socialist transformation' (2001: 159). After the sudden death of Berlinguer, Alessandro Natta became the leader from 1984 to 1988, a period during which 'the PCI failed to respond with sufficient alacrity or intellectual rigour. In whole areas of modern life – the family, consumption, the new service sector – the party had nothing much to say. After losing electoral ground for nearly a decade, its militants were getting increasingly desperate' (ibid.). This incapability of PCI to respond to the changes in society and to relate to people reflects the generalised crisis that the European left experienced in and after the 1980s.

The morning after giving a momentous speech during a political debate on television, Communist MP Michele Apicella has a car accident, as a consequence of which he suffers from amnesia. It is the eve of a general election, and Michele, who is also a sportsman, goes to Acireale, in Sicily, with his water polo team to play the last match of the league. The whole film takes place in and around the swimming pool, during a surreal, never-ending match, where various characters talk to Michele and seek his opinion – a union man; two enraged electors; a catholic; an old comrade from his years in the extra-parliamentary left; another old acquaintance, a Fascist; and a badly informed journalist who interviews him. Slowly, fragments of memories painfully re-emerge; Michele recollects events of his life and reconstructs his own identity. This process amounts for Michele to a true redescription, since he recounts stories from his past to himself and looks with different eyes at his deeds (as with the problematic memory of the Fascist schoolmate, who was forced by other students to walk with a sign around his neck saying 'I'm a Fascist, spit on me'). The fact that Michele redescribes and reinvents himself coincides with a redescription and reinvention of the same Moretti, an idea that finds confirmation in the following statement by the film-maker, in which he begins by talking of his character and ends up discussing himself:

> My character suffers from amnesia, because, rightly so, he wants to be different from that with which people identify him. Regardless of the memories or presents that all the characters offer me, it is as if they had seen all my previous films: as if they demanded that my character remained always the same, identical to my previous films. And I, Moretti-Michele, instead, try to make a different film. For instance in the scene of the Fascist in school with the sign around his neck: my character, Michele, exclaims: 'What a horrible scene!', like a director when he wants to cut a certain sequence from his film. (Moretti quoted in De Bernardinis 2001: 7)

All reviewers have highlighted how Michele's amnesia is a metaphor for the crisis of identity in the PCI generated by the long process that led to the fall of Communism in Eastern Europe. This theme is very strong in the film – what does it mean to be a Communist in Italy today, now that Communism appears to have been defeated by capitalism and has been proved to be conducive to antidemocratic, totalitarian societies? As the referee of the match suggests, 'You are a party to remake, you have disappeared, you float mid-air ... you lack identity, you have at least three souls. Who are you? You are a useless party. Innocuous.' Thus, the PCI at the end of the 1990s is seen not only as lacking identity, but also as innocuous, having lost the ideological aim of the revolution. While full of doubts, Michele does not resign himself to this description of the party; he admits that Italian Communists are confused, in crisis, but he is not 'one of those who believes that people are well, that the Communist party no longer has a raison d'être, that capitalism is a society that has proved to be able to solve its own contradictions'.

Michele, as Moretti has stated in an interview, is surrounded by words: 'Around my character, who suffers because he is alone, there's nothing other than words, rivers of words' (Moretti quoted in De Bernardinis 2001: 7). Prompted by all the characters who want him to speak, to talk to them, Michele also attempts verbal redescriptions of himself, of the Communist party and of the last decade of Italian history. All the interest surrounding him was caused by his televised speech, defined by one character as a speech of 'great courage', a 'very modern gesture', but the audacity and novelty of his discourse now escape Michele and all his verbalisations are inconsequential and weak utterances, repetitions of specks of concepts said and heard thousands of times: 'Our project to transform society…'; 'What has happened in this decade is an extraordinary process of transformation of our society, which is in part a consequence of the growth of the left. The dominant forces of Italian and international capitalism have imposed…'; 'The catholic question is one with that of the centre. We must work to conquer the centre.' It is the argument with the journalist, who in her article has put in his mouth her superficial phrases full of commonplace express-ions and clichés, which triggers Michele's reaction against meaningless expressions and prompts him to change his own discourse. Firstly, Michele rebels against dead metaphors and clichés that fail to describe effectively our reality: 'Negative trend. I never said it, I never thought it, I do not speak like that!'; secondly, he plans resistance: 'We must remain insensitive. We must be indifferent to today's words'; thirdly, he claims that his speech is different and that he has adopted a specific vocabulary: 'I am not one of those free, unrestrained people, outside all groupings, who talk freely – I am prejudiced'; finally, he realises the importance of finding a new vocabulary: 'We must invent a new language. To invent a new language, we must invent a new life.' It is only after this realisation that Michele can remember his momentous speech of the previous day: pressed by the insinuating questions of the journalists, Michele started to sing *E ti vengo a cercare*, a song by an intellectual, idiosyncratic Italian pop artist, Franco Battiato: 'This century which is ending / full of parasites with no dignity / urges me to be better / with more willpower.'

The verses of this song do not propose a novel, revolutionary description of society; rather, they express a generic dissatisfaction with the present and a desire for change. This song, thus, cannot be seen as an example of the 'new language' that will allow us to lead a 'new life'. Nevertheless, Moretti uses it as an indication of the necessity of finding such a language, one that – as he said in his real-life discourse in Piazza Navona – is able to speak 'to the head, the heart and the soul of the people'. Moretti, in fact, shows us how this song elicits a collective reaction from the public, which is otherwise indifferent to traditional political discourse – a growing phenomenon in most Western societies, including Italy. This is apparent when the scene moves from the memory of the speech in the TV studio, where Michele has begun to sing, to the present in the swimming pool, where all the public joins him in singing. In two other occasions in this film Moretti suggests that popular culture is better able to speak to the people than conventional political discourse: when the public in the swimming pool sings in chorus Bruce Springsteen's *I'm on Fire*; and when it follows with extreme participation the last sequences of *Doctor Zhivago*.

Michele's realisation of the necessity of forging a new language does not dispel his doubts nor answers all his questions – he remains a lonely, suffering character, who makes mistakes (as in the failed penalty in the dying seconds of the match) and feels frustrated (as testified by the accident that he causes while driving back to Rome). We will argue that, although Michele stops at the realisation of the necessity to create a new, more

Michele (Nanni Moretti) taking the penalty in *Palombella rossa* (1989)

effective vocabulary, one better able to speak to the people, Moretti does more and offers to the Italian moderate Communist community concrete new ways of describing itself. He does so by creating new metaphors – a speciality of Moretti, who through the years has put in Michele's mouth a series of expressions so powerful that they have immediately been adopted by Italian popular and political speech. We refer to phrases such as 'No, il dibattito no!' (No, not the debate! – *Io sono un autarchico*), which teased the left for having made discussion and self-analysis a sine qua non of the 1970s; and 'Continuiamo così, facciamoci del male' (Let's continue like this, let's harm ourselves! – *Bianca*), which has been used in all contexts, and has also specifically served as a metaphor of the lack of assertiveness of the Italian left. Both phrases continue to be used extraordinarily often in Italian political and mediatic discourses. In *Palombella rossa*, Moretti coined an expression that beautifully captures the problem of identity of the left in Italy and Western Europe in the late 1990s, as well as the frustrated desire of the PCI to govern the country: 'Siamo uguali, ma siamo diversi!' (We are the same, but we are different!). This phrase, which Michele repeats countless times with increasing despair, achieving a very comic effect, shows the inherent contradiction of a party that regards itself simultaneously as a parliamentary group and as a revolutionary force, that wants to be accepted as an official, moderate component of the democratic life of the country, but also maintain its specific history (be faithful to its past ideals, as Michele says in the film). Furthermore, the slogan 'We are the same, but we are different!' reflects the greatest challenge that left-wing European parties must face today – to engage with a vast number of diverse interests, movements and discourses, some of which are not political in the classical sense of the word, but which are nevertheless unified by their liberalism and anti-capitalism, and redefine (redescribe) them as socialist. As we have already argued above, the Italian as well as all mainstream left-wing parties in Europe not only are currently not engaging with these new movements and voices, but do not even show an understanding of the challenge, hence the continuous crisis of the left.

As a reaction to the crumbling of the Soviet bloc, and in order to be finally fully accepted as a legitimate political alternative, the PCI had to undergo a momentous transformation. On 12 November 1989, two days after the fall of the Berlin Wall, Achille Occhetto, the new leader of the PCI, announced that the party would change name; the expression *la cosa*, 'the thing', was generally adopted as a soubriquet for the nameless party.

Occhetto's contentious proposal had at least one positive effect, that of bringing the grassroots members back to the cells to take part in a discussion that released repressed rage, disconcert and confusion, but also passion and enthusiasm. Moretti decided to film these discussions, and the result is *La cosa*, a traditional documentary of montage, devoid of voice-over or captions (bar those indicating where the images were filmed: in Sicily, Genoa, Bologna, Naples, Turin, Milan, Tuscany and Rome). The concerns expressed by the comrades in *La cosa* are diverse, but some elements recur – for instance, the sense of crisis and confusion; the accusation that the party has lost contact with the masses; the reflection on the historical failure of socialism; and the admission of knowledge of and thus co-responsibility for the suffering of people under Communist regimes. A lucid comrade in the Milanese cell summarises the crisis of European socialism: given that the utopia of the revolution and the idea that all men are equal are gone, and that it has become clear that values such as sustainable development, pacifism and democracy are not 'made in Communism', what does it mean to be a Communist today?

Ideologically, *La cosa* is fully consistent with and a continuation of *Palombella rossa*, the emphasis being on the problem of redescribing 70 years of the political life of a community that identified with ideals now severely challenged, if not fading. By leaving the entire screen-time to the comrades' words, language is shown by Moretti to be the nub of the problem – to refound the party means to rediscuss it and historicise it. Moretti's film is a powerful indication of the necessity of doing this, of inventing a new vocabulary and, as a consequence, a new life for the community of people that once identified with the Communist utopia.

Depicting his alter ego Michele Apicella in *Palombella rossa* as an aphasic, amnesiac politician, who is verbally and physically attacked from all sides, and as a failed sportsman, Moretti derides his own political ambitions and denies himself authority. Similarly, in *Aprile* Moretti describes himself as an aphasic, impotent politician and film-maker. After the general election of 28 March 1994, won by the centre-right coalition led by Silvio Berlusconi, Nanni is invited by a French journalist to make a documentary about Italy: 'Your country must begin again to reflect on itself.' Nanni knows that it is important to make such documentary, but he clearly has no desire to and unsuccessfully tries to convince himself to shoot it. In the meantime, he resumes without conviction an old project, a musical on a Trotskyist pastry cook set in 1950s Italy (but then stops because 'I do not know if I am able to make a musical, I am not sure if I feel like it'), and films much more willingly his partner's pregnancy and the birth of his first child, Pietro. Two years after Berlusconi's victory another general election takes place: also on this occasion, Nanni is recalcitrant and his documentary about Italy does not seem to progress. Every time he sets out to film something, he remonstrates: 'Yes, but I am a little ashamed, I do not feel like it at all, but I must do it, but I do not feel like it,' and again: 'I do not feel much like shooting today. Today I will do nice takes, important ones, yes, even if I am a little ashamed. I should find the way to shoot without being seen. Anyway, I am in good shape today' (as if he were still Michele Apicella, the water polo player). When he interviews Corrado Stajano, an intellectual who refused to run for the second time with PDS, he complains instead: 'I am not in good shape today,' again using a sport metaphor. When he interviews Albanian refugees just landed in Brindisi he simply moans: 'I am not able!' This impotency comes across as lack of clarity, or even as utter confusion, as can be seen in the humorous episode in which he describes his intentions to his collaborators on the minivan: 'With this documentary I want to say what I think, without though provoking the right-wing spectators, because it really does not interest me, but without trying to convince them, I do not want to convince anybody, but even without pampering the left-wing spectators, but I want to say what I think, and how can one say what he thinks in a documentary? And, above all, what do I think?'

Nanni's unwillingness to make a documentary about Italy, and his claim to not know what he thinks, is consistent with his position as a liberal ironist. His reluctance, accompanied by an often expressed feeling of shame, testifies to Moretti's awareness of the contradiction inherent in left-wing political cinema: to discredit authority while constructing a discourse that is believed to be true, and that, thus, becomes itself an authority. Moretti wants to make a documentary about Italy, but would like to 'find the way of shooting without being seen' – a rather surprising statement for a film-maker who only films himself. He is ashamed of going public, of invoking for himself the authority that he debunks in others, of claming to know a truth that is hidden to others. Not surprisingly, Nanni seems much more at ease when filming his private life, and he is almost unable to stop videoing his son. Furthermore, the choice of using the form of the diary for his documentary can be seen as his desire to avoid going public, to remain in the dominion of private autobiography, in order to keep away from the mistakes he reproaches in others.

As Moretti himself noticed, this contradiction is even greater since the documentary is made in the end, and successfully so:

> Paradoxically, it may be that the meaning of the film is the opposite of what the letter expresses. Undoubtedly, the outcome of the film is different from what I apparently say in the film. The result is that, with my insecurities, my manias – the cappuccinos, the *latte macchiati* – my escapes from the locations of the documentary, I pretended to distance myself from my topic. In reality, instead, I recounted to the spectators some years of this country, in my own way, and above all I expressed my feelings on this country in the course of time. (Moretti quoted in De Bernardinis 2001: 16)

The success of Moretti's film in political terms can be once again measured by its ability to produce discourse – not only in the sense of the debates it provoked after its screening at the Venice Film Festival and its theatrical release, but also because it offered a new linguistic expression that immediately entered the popular and political speech in Italy. Watching Berlusconi accusing the Italian magistrates of being politicised on *Porta a Porta*, a popular evening programme on the state television channel RAI1 devoted to current political and social issues, Nanni invokes the reaction of Massimo D'Alema, then leader of PDS, who sits speechless in the studio and does not object to Berlusconi's criticism of the judges: 'D'Alema, react, say something, react, say something, answer, say something left-wing, say something even not left-wing, something civilised!' The phrase caught on and, as D'Alema himself admitted, 'stuck' to the politician. Even more importantly, 'Say something left-wing!' has become a truly new metaphor that continues to circulate in political discourse. Recently, the newspaper *la Repubblica* has included it in a small dictionary of the new phrases, terms and slogans that have characterised the last decades (Somaschini 2002: 28). The power of this phrase to be a new metaphor for the redescription of old concepts can be measured by its longevity – introduced in 1998, it is still very frequently used today, for instance in the debate on the crisis of the left in Italy raised by Moretti's speech in Piazza Navona, but also by the growth of protest movements on themes such as the reforms of the justice system, the education system, labour law and immigration law sought by the second Berlusconi government. The fecundity of Moretti's metaphor is due to its ability to offer a novel redescription of a community that is in crisis because of its inability to continue to describe itself using an out-of-date vocabulary. If a community is formed, as Rorty suggests, by 'speakers of a common language' (Rorty 1989: 59), what happens when the old metaphors (expressions such as 'revolutionary', 'anti-capitalist', 'dictatorship of the proletariat', 'anti private ownership', etc.) are no longer able to describe the community?

Moretti's work is politically incisive precisely because it offers to the moderate and liberal left-wing community new ways of describing itself. Being left-wing in Italy today means, Moretti suggests, to be indignant in the face of anti-democratic attacks on the independence of the magistrates like the one led by Berlusconi, of delirious attempts to dismember the Republic, such as the one carried out by Umberto Bossi's Northern League, but also in the face of the absence of the leaders of the left from the beach of Brindisi; it means not to be 'one of those who believes that people are well, that capitalism is a society that has proved to be able to solve its own contradictions'; it means to be prepared to retell and redescribe the history of one's own community with cruel irony; it means to demystify ideology and authority in all its forms, including one's own; it means to be able to react, to say something, it does not matter if it is left-wing, something civilised is enough. In short, it means a great number of different discourses that the left is failing to seize and organise into the new socialist project.

This redescription of the ex-Communists, or better of the moderate left-wing community, is in part problematic; for instance, some of its elements – the will to defend basic bourgeois freedoms, such as free press and speech – do not exclusively belong to the left. Nevertheless, we will claim that it is a very fitting description, which reflects both the crisis of the left in the last decades and the strengthening patterns of postmodern left-wing activism. The Italian and European left-wing are today characterised by a loss of ideology, by a rejection of dogmatism, an atomisation of activism and an individualisation of the political engagement, whose origin can be traced as far back as the aftermath of 1968. This individualism in political commitment is today more and more often counterbalanced by a shifting participation in group activism coinciding with specific campaigns – an activism that often claims to be non-ideological, as well as a replacement for party politics, which is widely perceived as failed and unsatisfactory. In the particular situation of contemporary Italy, in which more and more alarmed voices denounce a series of violations of basic rights and freedoms, it is not surprising that, when asking the leader of PDS to speak up against Berlusconi, Moretti straightforwardly identifies 'left-wing' with 'civilised'.

Moretti's political discourse is thus simple (it is a post-dogmatic liberal discourse that begins with self-criticism and that puts anti-Fascism at its heart), but is also incisive, all the more so because Moretti does not put himself forward as a figure of authority – he knows of course that he has become an authority, but he is ashamed of it. This shame translates into a firm severity – with himself, with others, and with cinema – a severity that Federica Villa has recognised in Moretti's films in the form of an activity of 'subtraction' (cf. Villa 1999). This severity induces Moretti to a relentless, cruel (and, in this case, extremely sophisticated) redescription of himself, of his community, and of society at large. It also urges him to make films that lie outside the canon and the established practice, without cinematographic referents (and thus utterly autarchic), because, to borrow Villa's words, 'Nanni Moretti is an obsessively rigorous film-maker, who is ashamed, and we hope he will continue to be, to make films like everybody else' (Villa 1999: 66).

La sconfitta (1973)
Directed by: Nanni Moretti
Writing Credits: Nanni Moretti
Produced by: Nanni Moretti
Runtime: 26 min. (Super-8, colour)
Cast: Nanni Moretti (Luciano), Luca Codignola (the leader), Guido Ambrosino, Franco Moretti, Maurizio Flores d'Arcais, Sergio Tiroli, Emanuele Gerratana, Luigi Moretti, Paola Sposini.

Synopsis: *La sconfitta* addresses the political doubts and anxieties of Luciano, a young militant in the extra-parliamentary left. Images of Luciano's private life alternate with those of a protest rally against the Andreotti government, while we listen to excerpts of popular TV and radio programmes, such as quiz shows and sports news. The short ends with the protagonist who addresses the audience from behind the camera, but his words are not audible. Some sequences from *La sconfitta* are inserted as flashbacks in *Palombella rossa*.

Paté de bourgeois (1973)

Directed by: Nanni Moretti
Writing Credits: Nanni Moretti
Produced by: Nanni Moretti
Runtime: 26 min. (Super-8, colour)
Cast: Nanni Moretti, Mariella Gramaglia, Luca Codignola, Maurizio Flores d'Arcais, Fabio Traversa, Franco Moretti, Stefano Lariccia, Piero De Chiara, Mila Lentini, Alberto Flores d'Arcais.

Synopsis: A series of detached scenes, including Moretti, sitting on a WC, puts his Super-8 camera on its stand; two friends talk about their lives, without truly establishing a communication; off-screen commentary on the crisis of a couple by Moretti himself; images of a real-life religious procession in Rome. 'Paté de bourgeois' is the amalgamation of the expressions 'paté de fois gras' and 'épater le bourgeois'.

Come parli, frate? (1974)

Directed by: Nanni Moretti
Writing Credits: Nanni Moretti
Produced by: Nanni Moretti.
Runtime: 52 min. (Super-8 colour)
Cast: Nanni Moretti (don Rodrigo), Lorenza Codignola (Lucia), Giorgio Viterbo (Renzo), Vincenzo Vitobello (fra Cristoforo), Fulvia Fazio (Agnese), Beniamino Placido (Conte Zio), Corrado Sannucci (Padre provinciale), Stefano Lariccia (il Griso), Fabio Traversa (a noble man), Luciana Agati, Fabio Sposini, Igor Skofic, Pietro Veronese.

Synopsis: A parody of Alessandro Manzoni's *I promessi sposi* through the comic adaptation of a selection of scenes from the novel.

Io sono un autarchico (1976)

Directed by: Nanni Moretti
Writing Credits: Nanni Moretti
Cinematography by: Fabio Sposini
Music by: Franco Piersanti
Film Editing by: Nanni Moretti
Produced by: Nanni Moretti
Runtime: 95 min. (Super-8, later blown up to 16 mm)

Cast: Nanni Moretti (Michele), Simona Frosi (Silvia, his wife), Andrea Pozzi (Andrea, their son), Fabio Traversa (Fabio, the director), Giorgio Viterbo (Giorgio, the teacher), Paolo Zaccagnini (Paolo), Luciano Agati (Giuseppe), Guido Valesini (the doctor), Beniamino Placido (the critic), Lori Valesin, Benedetta Bini, Alberto Flores d'Arcais, Luigi Moretti, Lucio Ravasini, Mauro Fabretti, Roberto Pizza, Franco Moretti, Alberto Abruzzese, Paolo Flores d'Arcais, Stefano Bergesio, Stefano Brasini, Andrea Parlatore, Fabio Sposini, Piero Galletti, Enrico Proietti.

Synopsis: Michele and his wife Silvia split up and their child Andrea remains temporarily with his father in his apartment in Rome. Michele, who is unemployed and receives a regular check from his father, is involved by his friend Fabio in an avant-garde theatre show. After the terrible experience at a training camp for the actors, the group begins to rehearse in a cellar. In the meantime, one of the actors, Giorgio, who is secretly in love with a neighbour on whom he spies from the window, finds a job as a substitute teacher outside Rome; Fabio, the director, contacts a famous critic hoping for a review; and Michele tries unsuccessfully to patch up his relationship with Silvia. The critic does attend the premiere, but in his subsequent dialogue with Fabio he avoids any mention of the show. After the last performance, Fabio tries unsuccessfully to involve the audience in a debate; none of the characters has resolved his problems, and the group splits up in an atmosphere of disappointment and lack of achievement. Michele meets Silvia one last time and hands over the child.

Ecce Bombo (1978)
Directed by: Nanni Moretti
Writing Credits: Nanni Moretti
Cinematography by: Giuseppe Pinori
Design by: Massimo Razii
Music by: Franco Piersanti
Film Editing by: Enzo Meniconi
Sound by: Franco Borni
Produced by: Filmalpha/Alphabeta
Runtime: 100 min.
Cast: Nanni Moretti (Michele), Luisa Rossi (his mother), Glauco Mauri (his father), Lorenza Ralli (Valentina, his sister), Fabio Traversa (Mirko),

Paolo Zaccagnini (Vito), Piero Galletti (Goffredo), Lina Sastri (Olga), Susanna Javicoli (Silvia), Carola Stagnaro (Flaminia), Maurizio Romoli (Cesare), Cristina Manni (Cristina), Simona Frosi (Simona), Giorgio Viterbo (Telecalifornia speaker), Luigi Moretti (the unemployed actor), Age (teacher), Mauro Fabretti, Maurizio De Taddeo (two students), Cristiano Gentili (Alvaro Rissa, the poet), Vincenzo Vitobello (the 'friend of the Ethiopian'), Giampiero Mughini (the intellectual), Andrea Pozzi, Alberto Abruzzese, Benedetta Bini, Augusto Minzolini, Filippo La Porta, Pier Farri, Luciano Agati, Nadia Fusini, Francesca Ghiotto, Roberto De Lellis, Guido Parlatore, Giampiero Lombardo, Carla Taviani, Maria Bufalini.

Synopsis: Four friends – Goffredo, Mirko, Vito and Michele – hang out together; often bored, they spend long hours in the bar. Michele lives with his family; he is in open conflict with his estranged father, seems ashamed of his mistreated mother, and would like to have complete control of the education of his younger sister, Valentina. The four friends decide to set up male-only self-analysis sessions; together they discuss memories of their youth and various personal problems, organise trips outside Rome, waste time. In the meantime, Michele goes out with Silvia, who works in the cinema, but often teases her for the poor quality of the films in which she is involved. He is offended when she goes to shoot outside Rome, despite his remonstrations, and their relationship ends. Michele then seduces Flaminia, the wife of Cesare, a new friend who joins the group. Sequences devoted to Michele's love life and family life alternate with images of the self-analysis sessions, and with those relating to an independent radio station in which Vito works, and which receives the phone calls of lonely listeners. In the meantime, Michele gives grinds to two high-school students, who then fail their final year exams. When all his friends leave Rome for the Summer holidays, Michele remains alone. Desperate for company, he starts going out again with an old flame, but the relationship does not work out. Eventually, the group splits up, and Mirko decides to join a more structured commune. One evening the friends, together with a large number of other young people in the city, decide to go to visit Olga, Mirko's schizophrenic friend, but they are all sidetracked on their way to her apartment. Michele, who initially had decided not to go, is the only one of them who actually visits her and the film ends with the two characters looking at each other, in silence.

Sogni d'oro (1981)

Directed by: Nanni Moretti
Writing Credits: Nanni Moretti
Cinematography by: Franco Di Giacomo
Design by: Giovanni Sbarra
Music by: Franco Piersanti
Film Editing by: Roberto Perpignani
Sound: Franco Borni
Produced by: Renzo Rossellini per Operafilm/Raiuno
Runtime: 105 min.
Cast: Nanni Moretti (Michele Apicella), Piera Degli Espositi (his mother), Laura Morante (Silvia), Alessandro Haber (Gaetano), Nicola Di Pinto (Nicola), Claudio Spadaro (Claudio), Remo Remotti (Freud), Miranda Campa (Freud's mother), Sabina Vannucci (Freud's daughter), Gigio Morra (Gigio Cimino), Giovanna De Luca (his wife), Giampiero Mughini (presenter), Chiara Moretti (presenter), Dario Cantarelli, Tatti Sanguinetti, Sahra Di Nepi, Oreste Rotundo, Mario Cipriani, Adriana Pecorelli, Marco Colli, Alberto Abruzzese, Mario Monaci Toschi, Fabrizio Beggiato, Luca Silvestri, Massimo Garzia, Vincenzo Salemme, Cinzia Lais; the troupe of *Freud's Mother*: Mario Garriba, Massimo Milazzo, Luigi Moretti (the producer), Cristina Manni, Memmo Giovannini, Giovanni Di Gregorio, Maria D'Incoronato, Alessio Gelsini.

Synopsis: Michele Apicella is a successful film-maker, labelled by the critics as the director for the young generation. At debates and round table discussions, Michele is regularly attacked by a 'chameleonic' critic of his cinema who, wearing a different outfit each time, condemns his films for being out of reach of simple people such as a shepherd from Abruzzo, a labourer from Lucania, or a housekeeper from Treviso. Michele, who lives with his mother, a secondary school teacher, is writing the screenplay of his next film, entitled 'Freud's Mother', the story of Freud (or of a madman who believes he is Freud), represented as an old man who still lives with his mother and behaves with her as if he were a small child. Michele, who finds it very difficult to concentrate on his work, is constantly harassed by two brothers who want to become his assistants, and rudely tries to shake them off. He has contact only with Gaetano, a depressed fellow director who has not made one film in the last six years. In his dream life, Michele imagines himself a teacher and having a love story with a beautiful and enigmatic student, Silvia. When the film goes into production, Michele accepts the two brothers as assistants, but tries to dissuade them from becoming directors themselves. He is very self-centred and exigent and has difficult relationships with all the cast, including his producer, who is also producing a musical about Vietnam by Gigio Cimino, a new director whom Michele despises. The two rival directors are the competitors in a trash TV game in which they must win the favour of the public – Cimino wins and Michele is humiliated. At another debate, a shepherd from Abruzzo, a labourer from Lucania, and a housekeeper from Treviso come to defend Michele from the usual accusations of intellectualism. Michele's new film is finally ready and is presented to the critics, whom Michele welcomes by saying 'This is my best film!' While at dinner with Silvia, the woman in his dreams, Michele transforms into a werewolf and chases her into a wood.

Bianca (1983)

Directed by: Nanni Moretti
Writing Credits: Nanni Moretti, Sandro Petraglia
Cinematography by: Luciano Tovoli
Design by: Giorgio Luppi, Marco Luppi
Music by: Franco Piersanti
Film Editing by: Mirco Garrone
Sound by: Franco Borni
Produced by: Faso Fil/Reteitalia
Runtime: 95 min.
Cast: Nanni Moretti (Michele Apicella), Laura Morante (Bianca), Roberto Vezzosi (head of police), Dario Cantarelli (schoolmaster), Remo Remotti (Siro Siri), Vincenzo Salemme (Massimiliano), Enrica Maria Modugno (Aurora), Claudio Bigagli (Ignazio), Margherita Sestito (Maria), Giorgio Viterbo (History teacher), Giovanni Buttafava (teacher), Luigi Moretti (psychologist), Mario Monaci Toschi (Edo), Matteo ago (Matteo), Virginie Alexandre (Martina), Alberto Bracco, Marie Christine Vandeneede, Mauro Fabretti, Nicola di Pinto, Gianfelice Imparato, Daniele Luchetti, Fabrizia Frezza, Angelo Barbagallo, Inigo Lezzi, Silvia Moretti, Maxime Alexandre, Frederique Alexandre, Henri Alexandre, Mario Garriba, Giovanna De Luca, Valerio Berruti.

Synopsis: Michele Apicella, a maths teacher, moves to a new apartment and begins his career at the Marilyn Monroe School. His new neighbours, whom he studies from his terrace, include Siro Siri, a mature man who likes being surrounded by young women, and Massimiliano and Aurora, a couple who argue constantly. Having found a way of getting into their apartment, Michele steals their pictures and files them in an archive of biographical details of the people he knows. The Marilyn Monroe School is unusual: the office of the schoolmaster is dominated by a poster of Dean Martin and Jerry Lewis; in the classrooms, the photograph of the president of the Italian Republic is replaced by that of the goalkeeper of the Italian football team; the students have at their disposal a bar with pinball and slot-machines; the history teacher, a favourite of the schoolmaster, lectures on the life of a contemporary Italian songwriter, using as teaching support the juke-box in the classroom; and a psychologist is always available to assist the teachers, rather than the students. Michele, who is not at ease in this environment, is nevertheless immediately attracted to Bianca, the new French teacher.

One day watching from his terrace he discovers that his neighbour Aurora betrays her partner. The morning after, Aurora is found dead. A police inspector interrogates Michele and, having noticed some abnormalities in his behaviour, begins to suspect him. In the meantime, Michele begins a difficult relationship with Bianca, and appears to be more and more obsessed by harmony in the couples he knows. After having tried without success to convince his friends Ignazio and Maria not to break up, Michele finds out that they have new partners. Once again, they are found dead. Lying, Bianca tells the police that she spent the night with Michele, furnishing him with an alibi – in truth, Michele had already left Bianca, because, as he told her, he did not want to suffer. The abnormalities in his behaviour multiply, until he gives himself up to the police, and confesses to being the murderer, accusing his peers of not having offered him a model of harmony and happiness to follow.

La messa è finita (1985)

Directed by: Nanni Moretti
Writing Credits: Nanni Moretti, Sandro Petraglia
Cinematography by: Franco Di Giacomo
Design by: Amedeo Fago, Giorgio Bertolini
Music by: Nicola Piovani
Film Editing by: Mirco Garrone
Sound by: Franco Borni

Produced by: Faso Film

Runtime: 94 min.

Cast: Nanni Moretti (Don Giulio), Margarita Lozano (his mother), Ferruccio De Ceresa (his father), Enrica Maria Modugno (Valentina, his sister), Marco Messeri (Saverio), Darlo Cantarelli (Gianni), Roberto Vezzosi (Cesare), Vincenzo Salemme (Andrea), Eugenio Masciari (Antonio, the ex-priest), Luisa De Santis (Lucia, his wife), Pietro De Vico, Giovanni Buttafava, Luigi Moretti (the judge), Mauro Fabretti, Francesco Di Giacomo, Antonella Fattori, Carlina Torta, Inigo Lezzi, Salidro De Santis, Bianca Pesce, Mario Monaci Toschi, Anna Cesareni, Oreste Rotundo, Conchita Airoldi, Silvia Moretti, Stefano Viali, Massimo Milazzo, Mariella Valentini.

Synopsis: After spending ten years as a priest in the island of Ventotene, Don Giulio returns home, having been assigned to a small parish in Rome. Almost immediately he discovers that he is out of tune with his parishioners, his friends, even his own family. He does not understand their problems, he cannot identify with their choices. The priest he came to replace had married a woman and had a child with her, and stayed on to live near the church, to the disappointment of Giulio, who regards him as a great sinner. Of his friends, Saverio, after breaking up with his partner, does not want to go out or see anybody; Andrea is awaiting trial accused of affiliation to a terrorist group; and Cesare wants to become a priest for reasons that Giulio deems to be wrong. Furthermore, his sister Valentina broke up with her estranged partner and wants to abort the baby she is expecting; and his father leaves his wife for a much younger woman, a friend of Valentina, and moves out. Don Giulio tries to help them all, but is also annoyed by them and often reacts with intolerance to their problems. He is particularly shaken by his father's decision. His only consolation is to spend some time with the family of the ex-priest, which paradoxically has revealed to be closer to the model of the Holy Family than any other one he knows. One day, he learns by phone that his mother has committed suicide. After this event, that annihilates Giulio, Cesare decides to give up his intention of becoming a priest and to marry instead. Don Giulio celebrates the wedding and announces his decision to leave Rome and go to a small church in Patagonia, where people might need his help. He smiles when he sees his family and friends dancing together to the tune of an Italian song, *Ritornerai* (You will return).

Palombella rossa (1989)

Directed by: Nanni Moretti
Writing Credits: Nanni Moretti
Cinematography by: Giuseppe Lanci
Music by: Nicola Piovani
Film Editing by: Mirco Carrone
Sound by: Franco Borni
Design by: Giancarlo Basili
Produced by: Nanni Moretti and Angelo Barbagallo for Sacher Film, Nella Banfi, Palmyre Film, Rai Uno, So.Fin.A.
Distribution: Titanus
Runtime: 89 min.
Cast: Nanni Moretti (Michele Apicella), Asia Argento (Valentina, his daughter), Silvio Orlando (Mario, coach of the Monteverde team), Mariella Valentini (the journalist), Alfonso Santagata, Claudio Morganti (two enraged electors), Eugenio Masciari (referee), Mario Patané (Simone, the Catholic), Luigi Moretti (the trade union man), Fabio Traversa (the old friend), Antonio Petrocelli (the Fascist), Imre Budavari (Hungarian player – himself), Mauro Maugeri (coach of the Acireale team), Giovanni Buttafava (psychoanalist, referee's spiritual leader), Raoul Ruiz (Simone's spiritual leader), Remo Remotti (ex-athlet, Mario's spiritual leader), Mario Schiano, Gabriele Ceracchini, Luisanna Pandolfi, Marco Messeri, Franco Bernini, Carlo Mazzacurati, Daniele Luchetti, Mario Monaci Toschi, Telemaco Mareoccia.

Synopsis: Michele Apicella, MP of the PCI (Italian Communist Party) and a player for the Monteverde waterpolo team, has a car accident, as a result of which he loses his memory. He goes to Sicily with his team for a match against Acireale, which will decide who wins the league. The whole film takes place in and around the swimming pool, during the never-ending match. Slowly, by talking to the other players and to people who come to see him, who recall fragments of his past, Michele reconstructs his identity, but still cannot remember the content of the momentous speech that he gave on television the night before. Among the people who talk to him are: a trade union man who reflects on the evolution of Italian politics; two edgy voters who admired his speech and seek Michele's approval; the match referee, who accuses Michele's party of having at least two souls and of being ineffective; a Catholic who insists on convincing Michele that they are the same and have the same convictions, and who introduces him to his spiritual leader; a journalist who interviews Michele and upsets him with her lack of professionalism and her stereotypical speech; two old acquaintances, a comrade from his activist days and a Fascist student who was forced to walk around with a sign around his neck saying 'I am a fascist, spit on me'. Michele struggles to recompose his identity, stares intensely at his photograph on his team's membership, and remembers unhappy moments of his childhood; at times he even wonders whether his memories are true or not. With his teenage daughter Valentina and many other people at the swimming pool he eagerly watches scenes from David Lean's *Doctor Zhivago*. Finally, while he is waiting to take the penalty that would give his team the victory, Michele remembers his speech of the night before, when he began to sing an Italian pop song (*E ti vengo a cercare,* by Franco Battiato). Michele misses the penalty, and when in the changing room with the rest of the team he complains that he expected more, not from the match but from life. Returning to Rome by car with his daughter, he thinks with increasing despair about the paradox of the PCI, which is – as he says – like the other parties, but different, and loses control of the car. In a dream-like sequence, Michele and his daughter leave the crashed car and climb a hill, walking towards a paper-pulp sun, along with many others, including Michele as a child and his mother.

La cosa (1990)

Directed by: Nanni Moretti
Cinematography by: Alessandro Pesci, Giuseppe Baresi, Roberto Cimatti, Riccardo Gambacciani, Cherardo Gossi, Angelo Strano
Film Editing by: Nanni Moretti
Sound by: Ugo Celani, Carlos Alberto Bonaudo, Ruggero Manzoni, Roberto Serra
Produced by: Angelo Barbagallo and Nanni Moretti for Sacher Film
Broadcasted on Rai3 on 6 March 1990
Runtime: 59 min.

Synopsis: *La cosa* is made up of filmed debates, between grassroots members of PCI, on the change of name of the party proposed by its then leader Achille Occhetto after the fall of the Berlin Wall in 1989. A traditional documentary of montage, *La cosa* is devoid of voiceover or captions, bar those indicating where the images were filmed: Francavilla (Sicily); San Giovanni a Teduccio (Campania); Ca' Nuova (Genoa); Bolognina (Bologna); Carrozzerie Mirafiori (Turin); Milano Lambrate; San Casciano di Val di Pesa (Tuscany); Roma Testaccio.

Caro diario (*Dear Diary*, 1994)
Directed by: Nanni Moretti.
Writing Credits: Nanni Moretti.
Cinematography by: Giuseppe Lanci
Design by: Marta Maffucci
Music by: Nicola Piovani
Film Editing by: Mirco Garrone
Sound by: Franco Borni
Produced by: Nanni Moretti, Angelo Barbagallo per Sacher Film
Runtime: 101 min.
Cast: Nanni Moretti (himself), Renato Carpentieri (Gerardo), Antonio Neiwiller (the mayor of Stromboli), Moni Ovadia (Lucio in Alicudi), Carlo Mazzacurati (the film critic), Mario Schiano (the Prince of dermatologists), Valerio Magrelli (first dermatologist), Sergio Lambiase (second dermatologist), Conchita Airoldi (resident of Panarea), Raffaella Lebbroni e Marco Paolini (first couple in Salina), Claudia della Seta e Lorenzo Alessandri (second couple in Salina), Serena Nono, Jennifer Beals, Alexandre Rockwell, Italo Spinelli.

Synopsis: *Dear Diary* is structured as three 'chapters', 'In Vespa' ('On My Vespa'), 'Isole' ('Islands'), and 'Medici' ('Doctors'). In 'On My Vespa' Nanni rides through Rome's deserted streets in the middle of August. Wearing helmet and dark glasses, he goes to see different areas of the city and fantasises about buying and restructuring penthouses. He 'dances' on his Vespa, and confesses that since he saw Adrian Lyne's *Flashdance* he always wanted to learn to dance. He watches with envy and delight a group of dancers at an outdoor Latin music concert, and later meets Jennifer Beals and her partner Alexander Rockwell in the street and talks to them about his obsession. When he is not on his Vespa, Nanni goes to the cinema. He dislikes an Italian film he sees, and dissociates himself from its protagonists, who were politically active in the 1970s and who comment on their current failure and embitterment, and is upset by the gory violence of an American movie, *Henry: Portrait of a Serial Killer*. Nanni sees himself at the bedside of a critic who wrote a positive review of this film, and forces him to listen to his own fanatical prose. Back on his Vespa, Nanni decides to go to the site of the murder of Pier Paolo Pasolini, which he had never visited before. The camera follows him in a long sequence that closes on the crumbling 'monument' to Pasolini.

At the beginning of 'Islands' we find Nanni travelling by ferry to the Eolie Islands; he intends to spend some time with his friend Gerardo, a Joyce scholar, who moved to Lipari eleven years before. In a bar in Lipari, Nanni sees a piece of an old film on TV. Gerardo scorns his friend, maintaining that he himself has not watched any television in the last 30 years. Not finding the peace and quiet which would allow them to work, Nanni and Gerardo move incessantly from one island to the next. In the course of their trip, Gerardo comes into contact with television and quickly becomes an avid viewer of soap operas and programmes of popular entertainment. In Salina they discover that the island is full of one-child families in which the parents obsessively look after their offspring, with the result that the island is subtly dominated by children. In Stromboli they meet the mayor, who wants to modernise the island by installing a permanent soundtrack by Ennio Morricone and lighting by Vittorio Storaro. When in Vulcano, which they reach after running away from the fashionable and vulgar Panarea, Gerardo sends Nanni to ask a group of American tourists for information on the future episodes of *The Bold and The Beautiful*; and when in Alicudi, the island without electricity, he first writes a letter to the Pope, whom he berates for having excommunicated soap operas, and then runs away from the island, shouting that Enzensberger and Popper are utterly wrong and that television is not bad for adults nor for children.

In 'Doctors' Nanni recounts his own experience with Hodgkin's disease, a curable form of cancer. The whole episode is told in a flashback: first we meet him in a bar in Rome, writing his diary at a table. He declares that, having kept the prescriptions of all the medicines, as well as having taken notes of all his conversations with doctors, 'nothing in this chapter is invented'. The sequence which follows is an excerpt from the last session of Moretti's real-life chemotherapy treatment. The rest of the episode is concerned with Nanni's interminable ordeal, searching for a doctor who will finally understand the causes of his tormenting itch. In tandem with the many examinations (he is examined among others by three different doctors at the Institute of Dermatology; by the assistant to the most famous dermatologist in Rome, know as 'the Prince'; by the 'Prince' himself; as well as by two Chinese doctors), Nanni is continuously prescribed massive amounts of medicines, special soaps, shampoos and creams, which neither heal nor improve his condition. Finally, it is a Chinese doctor who, alarmed by the patient's cough, suggests a chest X-ray, following which Nanni is prescribed a CAT scan that reveals the tumour. After the operation (which we are not shown), we find Nanni once again in the 'present' of the story, sitting at the table in the bar, writing his last comments and ready to have his breakfast.

L'unico paese al mondo (1994)

Directed by: Francesca Archibugi, Antonio Capuano, Marco Tullio Giordana, Daniele Luchetti, Mario Martone, Carlo Mazzacurati, Nanni Moretti, Marco Risi, and Stefano Rulli
Cinematography by: Alessandro Pesci
Film Editing by: Roberto Missiroli
Produced by: Angelo Barbagallo and Nanni Moretti
Runtime: 20 min.
Projected at the cinema Anteo, Milan, on 24 March 1994

Synopsis: A collective film denouncing the anomalous candidature of Silvio Berlusconi, owner of a media empire, in the general election of 1994. In his episode, Nanni rides his Vespa through the Parisian quarter of la Défense, observing that Berlusconi tried in vain to make it in France, and commenting on the differences between the Italian and French bourgeoisie.

Il giorno della prima di 'Close Up' (*Opening Day of 'Close-Up'*, 1996)

Directed by: Nanni Moretti
Cinematography by: Alessandro Pesci
Sound: Andrea Masciocchi, Bruno Pupparo
Produced by: Angelo Barbagallo and Nanni Moretti for Sacher Film
Runtime: 7 min.
Cast: Nanni Moretti, Fabia Bergamo, Paolo Di Virgilio, Paola Orfei, Fausto Polacco, Amleto Vitali.

Synopsis: Moretti appears in his role as manager of the Nuovo Sacher, his cinema theatre in Rome. He meticulously prepares the debut of Abbas Kiarostami's *Close-Up* by advertising the film in the press, checking which sandwiches are sold in the cinema, preparing his staff to answer the spectators' questions, and testing the volume of the sound with the projectionist. At night, he learns *Close-up*'s ticket sales, and those of the big American productions shown in other cinemas.

Aprile (1998)
Directed by: Nanni Moretti
Writing Credits: Nanni Moretti
Cinematography by: Peppe Lanci
Produced by: Angelo Barbagallo and Nanni Moretti for Sacher Film, Bac Film, in collaboration with Rai and Canal Plus
Runtime: 78 min.
Cast: Nanni Moretti, Pietro Moretti, Silvia Nono, Silvio Orlando, Agata Apicella Moretti, Nuria Schoenberg, Angelo Barbagallo, Renato De Maria.

Synopsis: After the general election of 28 March 1994, won by the centre-right coalition led by Silvio Berlusconi, Nanni is invited by a French journalist to make a documentary about Italy. Nanni knows that it is important to make such a documentary, but he clearly has no desire to do so and unsuccessfully tries to convince himself to shoot it. Two years after Berlusconi's victory another general election takes place: once again, Nanni is recalcitrant and his documentary about Italy does not seem to progress. In the meantime, he resumes without conviction an old project, a musical on a Trotskyist pastry cook set in 1950s Italy, and films much more willingly his wife Silvia's pregnancy. Nanni is excited about this event, but appears to be more nervous than Silvia. Shortly after the birth of his first child, Pietro, the centre-left coalition, Ulivo, wins the election. Nanni seems to retreat more and more into the private sphere; he consults a psychologist who helps him to define his role as a father, and he asks his mother how she coped with breastfeeding while working full time as a teacher. Since everybody around him expects him to make his documentary, he reluctantly goes to Venice to film Umberto Bossi's declaration of independence of the northern region, self-baptised as Padania, and later to Brindisi, in Puglia, to film the landing of a boat full of Albanian refugees, and complains about the absence of the leaders of the left on that occasion. The documentary is never finished.

On the day of his forty-third birthday he is given by a friend a measuring tape to measure how long is left for him to live. Nanni throws away all the newspaper clippings that he ever kept and which made him feel miserable, puts on a cape he never had the courage to wear and drives his Vespa to the set of the musical, where shooting has finally started.

La stanza del figlio (*The Son's Room*, 2001)
Directed by: Nanni Moretti
Writing credits: Nanni Moretti, Linda Ferri, Heidrun Schleef
Cinematography by: Giuseppe Lanci
Film Editing by: Esmeralda Calabria
Design by: Giancarlo Basili
Sound by: Alessandro Zanon
Music by: Nicola Piovani
Produced by: Angelo Barbagallo and Nanni Moretti for Sacher Film
Runtime: 98 min.
Cast: Nanni Moretti (Giovanni), Laura Morante (Paola), Jasmine Trinca (Irene), Giuseppe Sanfelice (Andrea), Sofia Vigliar (Arianna), Renato Scarpa (Headmaster), Roberto Nobile (Priest), Paolo De Vita (Luciano's Father), Roberto De Francesco (Record Store Clerk), Claudio Santamaria (Dive Shop Clerk), Antonio Petrocelli (Enrico), Lorenzo Alessandri (Filippo's Father), Alessandro Infusini (Matteo), Silvia Bonucci (Carla), Marcello Bernacchini (Luciano), Alessandro Ascoli (Stefano), Stefano Abbati (Patient); Giovanni's patients: Stefano Accorsi, Toni Bertorelli, Dario Cantarelli, Eleonora Danco, Claudia Della Seta, Luisa De Santis, Silvio Orlando.

Synopsis: Giovanni, a consultant psychoanalyst, lives in a nice apartment in Ancona with his wife, Paola, owner of a refined bookshop, and their two teenage children, Andrea and Irene. The family lives in complete harmony, the parents being deep in love with one another and affectionate and attentive towards their children. Giovanni often jogs with Andrea, and is only slightly concerned by the lack of competitiveness in his son, something which he considers odd in a boy of his age. Giovanni's studio is next to the apartment; he is very committed to his job and to his patients. The parents are only a little worried when Andrea and a schoolmate are accused of stealing a fossil from the school collection. The boy denies responsibility, but eventually confesses to his mother that they stole it as a joke, that they intended to put it back, but the fossil broke before they could replace it. One Sunday morning, Giovanni convinces Andrea to go jogging with him instead of going scuba diving with his friends, but their plan is changed by a phone call from a patient with suicidal tendencies, who asks Giovanni to visit him at home, something he reluctantly agrees to do. When he returns, Giovanni finds out that Andrea died accidentally during the dive. The family's harmony is destroyed. The tragedy is particularly hard to endure as the family is secular; but whereas both women externalise their grief, Giovanni tortures himself by continually going over the events of the fatal day, and ends up holding both himself and his patient responsible for Andrea's death. His relationship with his wife is endangered more and more; Giovanni even decides to give up his job, as he feels unable to maintain a professional attitude towards his patients. When she finds out that her son had a girlfriend, Arianna, whom he had briefly met at a Summer camp, Paola tries to contact her, and places all her hope in her. Arianna at first rejects the approach, then goes to visit the family. Arianna, who is accompanied by Stefano, perhaps her new boyfriend, is on her way to France. Giovanni, Irene and Paola drive Arianna and Stefano to a service station on the motorway, from where they intend to hitchhike; when Irene, Arianna and Stefano fall asleep in the car, Giovanni and Paola decide to drive on. They drive all night and in the morning they reach the border with France. For the first time since the tragedy, Giovanni and Paola are close once again. While Arianna and Stefano leave by bus, Giovanni, Irene and Paola take a stroll on the beach.

NOTES

1 For a concise discussion of the characteristics and history of autobiography see 'Autobiography' in *Encyclopaedia Britannica* (Chicago: William Benton, 1970).

2 However, it is worth noting that Jarman is not regarded as an ordinary film-maker, but rather as a painter who uses the medium of film.

3 Moretti's self-irony will be discussed in detail in chapter three (cf. the sections on 'Satire and its discontents' and on 'Existential irony').

4 Moretti's diary films evoke some of Zavattini's most radical theories, such as the shadowing (*pedinamento*) of a human being for a day, while filming all the things that happen to him or her (Moretti re-enacts the events in his own life rather that shooting them as they happen, but the two practices coexist in Zavattini's writings); the prophecy of a cinema freely made and controlled by 'normal' people, with light and inexpensive technical means, in order to convey their own opinions and give account of big and small

events, an idea that Zavattini promulgated in the 1960s with his utopian *Cinegiornali liberi* (Free Newsreels; notice that *Dear Diary*, in particular, in its fragmentation and division into miscellaneous episodes, could be seen as a *cinegiornale*, a newsreel; and also that Moretti in the diary films paints himself not as a well-known film-maker and intellectual but rather as a 'normal' person whom nobody recognises); finally, and most importantly, in the 1950s Zavattini claimed that the diary, intended as 'the attempt to subject to the judgement [of the spectator] oneself, the others and everything worth telling ... [is] the most complete and authentic expression of the cinema' (Zavattini 1979: 71–2). Moretti also shares with Zavattini an interest in the diaries of others. Zavattini initiated several different projects that included diaries that were to be written by other people; Moretti has produced seven films for television based on the diaries of ordinary people, the *Diari della Sacher* (*Sacher's Diaries*, 2001), which were presented at the 2001 Venice Film Festival and are, as Nanni intended, only the first of a longer series of filmed diaries.

5   Cf. Rorty (1989). For a discussion of postmodern irony see also Hutcheon (1989). We will engage more comprehensively with Rorty's theory of the 'liberal ironist' in chapter four.

CHAPTER THREE

1   We will analyse this question extensively in chapter four. Here it is worth reiterating that authority is one of the most important targets of Moretti's satire.

2   This is a well-known part of the vocabulary of the post-1968 liberal discourse on the modernisation of the Italian school.

3   On the association on the concept of detachment with irony cf. for instance Muecke 1980: 216 ff.

4   This is a position that Kierkegaard shares with Rorty.

5   Moretti played in the course of his career a film-maker, a teacher, a priest, an MP and now a psychoanalyst.

CHAPTER FOUR

1   Cf. our discussion of Moretti's humbleness in chapter one.

2   Although politically hostile to Berlusconi, *L'Espresso* paradoxically is part of

Berlusconi's editorial empire.

3   For an account of this debate see Casetti 1999: 184–203.

4   Cf. the analysis of John Ford's *Young Mr Lincoln* in Comolli & Narboni 1976.

5   For a discussion of the similarities between Moretti and these and other directors, see the introduction to this volume.

6   We have discussed at length the question of autobiography and of the distinction between Moretti and his filmic incarnations in chapter one.

BIBLIOGRAPHY

'Il sondaggio: Ulivo, il caso Moretti' (2002), *la Repubblica.it*, ysiwyg://20/http://www.repubblica.it/speciale/poll/casomoretti.html (Wednesday 6 February).

'Rutelli a Moretti: "Polemiche distruttive"' (2002), *la Repubblica.it*, ysiwyg://8/http://www.repubblica.it/online/politica/comme/rutelli/rutelli.html (Sunday 3 February)

'The Moment is Now. The Rebirth of Italian Cinema' (2002), *Economist.com*, 18 April.

Ang, I. (1992) 'Hegemony-in-trouble', in D. Petrie (ed) *Screening Europe* (London: BFI).

Argentieri, M. (1990) 'Io sono un autarchico', Rinascita, 18 February 1997, reprinted in P. Ugo & A. Floris (eds) *Facciamoci del male. Il cinema di Nanni Moretti* (Cagliari: CUEC)

Aspden, P. (1994) '*Caro diario* (Dear Diary)', *Sight & Sound*, December, 42-3.

Auty, M. (1979) '*Ecce Bombo*', *Monthly Film Bulletin*, July, 170.

Bly, R. (1990) *Iron John* (Longmead: Element Books).

Bonsaver, G. (2001–2002) 'The Egocentric Cassandra of the Left: Representations of Politics in the Films of Nanni Moretti', *The Italianist*, 21–2, 158–83.

____ (2002) 'Three Colours Italian', *Sight and Sound*, January, 28–30.

Bouquet, S. (2001) 'Le divan du père. *La Chambre du fils* de Nanni Moretti', *Cahiers du cinéma*, 557 (May), 24-6.

Bragaglia, C. (1999) 'Autobiografie e cari diari: Nanni Moretti e gli altri', *Annali d'Italianistica*, 17, 69–76.

Bronfenbrenner, U. (1972) 'The Changing Soviet Family', in Gordon, M. (ed) *The Nuclear Family in Crisis: The Search for an Alternative* (New York: Harper & Row).

Bufacchi, V. & S. Burgess (2001) *Italy Since 1989. Events and Interpretations* (Basingstoke & New York: Palgrave).

Cappabianca, A. (1990) 'Come parli frate?', *Filmcritica*, 248 (1974), 351–2, reprinted in P. Ugo & A. Floris (eds) *Facciamoci del male. Il cinema di Nanni Moretti* (Cagliari: CUEC).

Caporale, A. (2002) 'Dalla base una valanga di email. "Ha dato voce alla nostra rabbia"', *la Repubblica* (Monday 4 February).

Casetti, F. (1999) *Theories of Cinema, 1945–1995*, trans. F. Chiostri & E. Gard Bartolini-Salimbeni (Austin: University of Texas Press).

Censi, R. (1998) 'Michele-Giulio-Giovanni', *Cineforum*, 373 (April), 26-7.

Chodorow, N. J. (1991) *Femininities, Masculinities, Sexualities* (Lexington: The University Press of Kentucky).

Codelli, L. (1994) '*Journal intime*. Nanni Moretti, I, II, III', *Positif*, 399 (May), 6–8.

Comolli, J.-L. & J. Narboni (1976) 'Cinéma/Idéologie/Critique', *Cahiers du cinéma*, 216 (October 1969), reprinted in B. Nichols (ed) *Movies and Methods*, vol. 1 (Los Angeles: University of California Press).

Comuzio, E. (1993) 'Moretti a tu per tu con il pubblico', *Cineforum*, 329 (November), 62–3.

Cremonini, G. (1999) 'La forma comica del pensiero', in *Nanni Moretti*, Garage Cinema Autori Visioni (Turin: Paravia Scriptorium).

____ (2001) 'Diverso/uguale', *Cineforum*, 403, 10–12.

Cross, A. (1988) 'Neither either nor or: The perils of reflexive irony', in A. Hannay & G. D. Marino (eds) *The Cambridge Companion to Kierkegaard* (Cambridge: Cambridge University Press).

Cruciani, M. (2000) 'Da Michele a Nanni: un itinerario psicoanalitico nel cinema di Moretti', *Cinecritica*, 17 (January–March), 71–81.

D'Aquino, A. (2000) 'Caro Diario: A Modern Journey of Purification', *Rivista di Studi Italiani*, 2, 270–80.

Daney, S. (1995) *Il cinema e l'oltre* (Milan: Il Castoro).

De Bernardinis, F. (1998) *Nanni Moretti*, 3rd edn. (Milan, Il Castoro).

____ (2001) *Nanni Moretti*, 4th revised edn. (Milan, Il Castoro).

De Gregorio, C. (2002) 'L'ultimo urlo di Nanni. "Corteo inutile, siete perdenti"', *la Repubblica* (Sunday 3 February), 3.

De Lauretis, T. (1984) *Alice Doesn't. Feminism, Semiotics, Cinema* (London: The Macmillan Press).

Detassis, P. & M. Sesti (1989) 'Nanni Moretti et le noveau cinéma italienne', *Positif*, 346 (December), 10–13.

Detassis, P. (1986a) 'La messa è finita', *Cineforum*, 251 (January/February), 43–8.

____ (1986b) 'Pateticamente credo ancora nel cinema. Dichiarazioni di Nanni Moretti', *Cineforum*, 251 (January/February), 46–8.

Ehrenreich, B. (1995) 'The Decline of Patriarchy' in M. Berger *et al.* (eds) *Constructing Masculinity* (London: Routledge).

Engels, F. (1972) *The Origin of the Family, Private Property and the State* (London: Lawrence & Wishart).

Erikson, E. H. (1994) *Identity and the Life Cycle* (New York: Norton & Company).

Escobar, R. (1978) '*Ecce Bombo* di Nanni Moretti: una via d'uscita dalla crisi?', *Cineforum*, 176 (July/August), 430–6.

Everett, W. (1996) 'The autobiographical eye in European film', *Europa*, 1: 1, article 2. On-line: http://www.intellectbooks.com/europa/number1/everett.htm (20 November 2002).

Fadda, M. (1998) 'La nuova vita di un autarchico. *Aprile*', *Cineforum*, 373 (April), 22–5.

Fargier, J. P. (1978) '*Ecce Bombo*', *Cahiers du cinéma*, 290-1 (July/August), 21–2.

Fini, M. (1990) 'Torna a casa Nanni', *Pagina*, June 1984, reprinted in P. Ugo & A. Floris (eds) *Facciamoci del male. Il cinema di Nanni Moretti* (Cagliari: CUEC).

Fittante, A. (1998) 'Decostructing Nanni', in 'Dossier *Aprile*', *Segnocinema*, 91 (May–June), 6.

Fofi, G. (1990) 'Vitelloni 78', *Linus*, May 1978, reprinted in P. Ugo & A. Floris (eds) *Facciamoci del male. Il cinema di Nanni Moretti* (Cagliari: CUEC).

_____ (2001) 'Nanni, Gabriele e tutti quanti', *Lo straniero*, 15/16 (Spring), 220–1.

Fonzi, G. (1972) 'The new arrangement', in M. Gordon (ed) *The Nuclear Family in Crisis: The Search for an Alternative* (New York: Harper & Row).

Fornara, B. (2001) 'Il ladro e il padrone', *Cineforum*, 403, 3–6.

Fortichiari, V. (1992) 'Diario', in G. Moneti (ed) *Lessico Zavattiniano* (Venice: Marsilio).

Gallo, G. (2001) 'Italia, il paese dove si divorzia meno', *Corriere della Sera*, 8 August, 15.

Gibbins, J. R. & B. Reimer (1999) *The Politics of Postmodernity. An Introduction to Contemporary Politics and Culture* (London, Thousand Oaks, New Dehli: Sage).

Giddens, A. (1998). *The Third Way. The Renewal of Social Democracy* (Cambridge: Polity Press).

Gieri, M. (1995) *Contemporary Italian Film-making: Strategies of Subversion* (Toronto: University of Toronto Press).

Gili, J. A. (1987) 'Des films pour exorciser mes obsessions. Entretien avec Nanni Moretti', *Positif*, 311 (January), 14–18.

_____ (1989) 'Nous voudrions que ce soir ça se termine bien. Entertien avec Nanni Moretti', *Positif*, 346 (Decèmber), 16–21.

_____ (1991) 'Le rêveur éveillé. *Sogni d'oro*', *Postif*, 365–66 (July/Aug), 30–1.

_____ (1994) 'Entretien avec Nanni Moretti. Le plaisir de reconter plus librement', *Positif*, 399, May, 9–14.

Ginsborg, P. (1990) *A History of Contemporary Italy. Society and Politics 1943-1988* (London: Penguin Books).

_____ (2001) *Italy and Its Discontents. Family, Civil Society, State 1980-2001* (London: Penguin).

Giovannini, M., E. Magrelli & M. Sesti (1986) *Nanni Moretti* (Naples: Edizioni Scientifiche Italiane).

Godfrey, T. (1999) 'Diaries, or Why I Can't Write Them', in M. Heller (ed) *Diary* (Manchester: Cornerhouse).

Good, J. & I. Velody (eds) (1998) *The Politics of Postmodernity* (Cambridge: Cambridge University Press).

Gramsci, A. (1992) *Selection from the Prison Notebooks of Antonio Gramsci*, ed. and trans. by Q. Hoare & J. Nowell Smith (New York: International Publishers).

Hall, S. (1988) *The Hard Road to Renewal: Thatcherism and the Crisis of the Left* (London: Verso).

_____ (1992) 'The Question of Cultural Identity', in S. Hall, D. Held & T. McGrew (eds) *Modernity and its Futures* (Cambridge: Polity Press).

Heller, M. (ed.) (1999) *Diary* (Manchester: Cornerhouse).

Horrocks, R. (1994) *Masculinity in Crisis* (Houndmills: Basingstoke).

Hutcheon, L. (1989) *The Politics of Postmodernism* (London: Routledge).

Jackson, D. D. (ed) (1960) *The Etiology of Schizophrenia* (New York: Basic Books).

Jameson, F. (1993) 'From *Class and Allegory in Contemporary Mass Culture*: *Dog Day Afternoon* as a Political Film', in A. Easthope (ed) *Contemporary Film Theory* (Karlow: Longman).

Jousse, T. & N. Saada (1994) 'Entretien avec Nanni Moretti', *Cahiers du cinéma*, 479–80 (May), 55–61.

Jousse, T. (1994) 'Moretti ou Berlusconi', *Cahiers du cinéma*, 479–80 (May), 62–4.

_____ (1998) 'Docteur Nanni et Mister Moretti', *Cahiers du cinéma*, 524 (May), 70–1.

Joyard, O. & J. Larcher (2001) 'Nanni Moretti. La voie grave. Entretien avec Nanni Moretti', *Cahiers du cinéma*, May, 18–23.

_____ (2001) 'L'effacée volontaire. Entretien avec Laura Morante', *Cahiers du cinéma*, 557 (May), 26–7.

Kanter, R. M. (1972) 'Communes', in M. Gordon (ed.) *The Nuclear Family in Crisis: The Search for an Alternative* (New York: Harper & Row).

Kemp, P. (2002) 'The Son's Room', *Sight & Sound*, March, 56.

Kierkegaard, S. (1992a) *The Concept of Irony with Continual Reference to Socrates* (1841), trans. H. V. Hong (Princeton, NJ: Princeton University Press).

_____ (1992b) *Concluding Unscientific Postscript* (1846), trans. H. V. Hong and E. H. Hong (Princeton, NJ: Princeton University Press).

Kleinhans, C. (1998) 'Marxism and Film', in J. Hill & P. Church Gibson (eds) *The Oxford Guide to Film Studies* (New York, Oxford University Press).

Malanga, P. (1993) '*Caro diario*', *Duel*, 8 (December), 25–6.

Mallon, T. (1984) *A Book of One's Own* (London: Picador).

Marangi, M. (1999) 'Nanni '90 ovvero Caro Aprile', in *Nanni Moretti*, Garage Cinema Autori Visioni (Turin: Paravia Scriptorium).

Marchesi, S. (1999) 'Accumulazione e sviluppo in *Caro Diario*', *Annali d'Italianistica*, 17, 77–94

Marcus, M. (1996) '*Caro diario* and the cinematic body of Nanni Moretti', *Italica*, vol. 73, 2, 233-47, reprinted in M. Marcus (2002) *After Fellini. National Cinema in the Postmodern Age* (Baltimore and London: Johns Hopkins University Press).

Marlia, G. (1988) 'Riso amaro: cinema comico e società italiana degli anni 80', in G. Marlia (ed.) *Non ci resta che ridere. Testimonianze sul cinema comico italiano* (Montepulciano: Editori del Grifo).

Martini, E. (1989) 'Intervista a Nanni Moretti', *Cineforum*, 288 (October), 64–7.

_____ (1993) '*Caro diario*', *Cineforum*, 329 (November), 58–63.

_____ (2001) 'Il filo di Arianna', *Cineforum*, 403, 9–10.

Masi, S. (1984) '*Bianca* di Nanni Moretti', *Cineforum*, 234 (May), 45–50.

Masoni, T. (2001) 'Adagio moderato, pianissimo', *Cineforum*, 403, 12–13.

Mazierska, E. (2001) 'Miedzy upokorzeniem, nuda a meczenstwem – Jean-Luca Godarda portrety filmowcow', *Kwartalnik Filmowy* (Poland), Wiosna, 33, 111–22.

Merchant, W. M. (1972) *Comedy* (London: Methuen).

Mitchell, T. (1996) 'Berlusconi, Italian television and recent Italian cinema. Reviewing *The Icicle Thief*', *Film Criticism*, Fall, 13–33.

Moravia, A. (1990) 'Film sul film nel film', *L'Espresso*, 11 October 1981, reprinted in P. Ugo & A. Floris (eds) *Facciamoci del male. Il cinema di Nanni Moretti* (Cagliari: CUEC).

Morreale, E. (2001) 'Moretti e la malinconia', *Cineforum*, 403, 6–8.

Muecke, D. C. (1980) *The Compass of Irony* (London & New York: Methuen).

Mulvey, L. (1989) 'Visual Pleasure and Narrative Cinema' [1975], reprinted in L. Mulvey, *Visual and Other Pleasures* (Basingstoke, Hampshire & London: Macmillan).

Neale, S. & Krutnik, F. (1990) *Popular Film and Television Comedy* (London & New York: Routledge).

Osmolska-Metrak, A. (1994) 'Wloski pamietnik', *Kino*, Lipiec-sierpien, 18–20.

Pellizzari, L. (1999) 'Nanni Moretti. Il fragile spessore della vita', *Cineforum*, 389 (November), 67–8.

Pellizzari, L. (2001) 'La stanza della sinistra', *Cineforum*, 403, 14.

Pernod, P. (1989) 'Michele, le monde a besoin d'égotistes comme toi (*Palombella rossa*)', *Positif*, 346 (December), 14–16.

Philippon, A. (1986) 'Le grand inquisiteur', *Cahiers du cinéma*, 382 (April),

49–51.

_____ (1994) 'Stromboli, c'est pas fini', *Cahiers du cinéma*, 481 (June), 66–9.

Phillips, A. (1994) *On Flirtation* (London: Faber & Faber).

Pigoullié, J.-F. (1991) 'Pubblico di merda (*Sogni d'oro*)', *Cahiers du cinéma*, 442 (April), 68–9.

Pollock, G. (1980) 'Artists Mythologies and Media Genius, Madness and Art History', *Screen*, 21:3, 57-96.

Porro, M. (2001) 'Film e potere, classifica italiana. Primi Aldo, Giovanni e Giacomo', *La Repubblica*, 27 August, 27.

Porton, R. & Ellickson, L. (1995) 'Comedy, Communism, and pastry. An interview with Nanni Moretti', *Cineaste*, 1–2, 11–15.

Raczek, T. (1986) 'Boze peryferie', *Kino* (Poland), 6, 46–7.

Rascaroli, L. (2003) 'New voyages to Italy: postmodern travellers and the Italian road film', *Screen*, 44, 1, 71–91.

Rohmer, E. (1989) *The Taste for Beauty*, trans. C. Volk (Cambridge: Cambridge University Press).

Rorty, R. (1989) *Contingency, Irony and Solidarity* (Cambridge: Cambridge University Press).

Rosso, U. (2002) 'Moretti attacca, choc nell'Ulivo', *la Repubblica*, 3 February, 2.

Saada, N. & Toubiana, S. (1998) 'Pâtisserie, politique et paternité. Entretien avec Nanni Moretti', *Cahiers du cinéma*, 524 (May), 49–65.

_____ (1998) 'Week-end à Rome', *Cahiers du cinéma*, 524 (May), 48.

Saada, N. (1994) 'Et la vie continue…', *Cahiers du cinéma*, 479–80 (May), 51–4.

Samueli, A. (1994) 'L'unique pays au monde', *Cahiers du cinéma*, 479–80 (May), 66–7.

Sass, L. A. (1997) 'The consciousness machine: Self and subjectivity and modern culture' in U. Neissen & D. A. Jopling (eds) *The Conceptual Self in Context. Culture, Experience, Self-Understanding* (Cambridge: Cambridge University Press).

Sesti, M. (1999) 'La bella imagine. *Aprile*', in *Nanni Moretti*, Garage Cinema Autori Visioni (Turin: Paravia Scriptorium).

Solanas, F. & O. Getino (1976), 'Towards a Third Cinema', reprinted in B. Nichols (ed) *Movies and Methods*, vol. I (Berkeley, University of California Press).

Somaschini, A. (2002) 'E voi, siete burka o girotondini? La fabbrica delle parole del futuro', *la Repubblica*, 10 April, 28.

Sontag, Susan (1979) *Illness as Metaphor* (London: Allen Lane).

Strauss, F. (1989) 'Je suis un autarcique', *Cahiers du cinéma*, 425 (November), 30.

Thirard, L. (1987) 'Du bon usage de la soutane. Sur *La messe est finie*', *Positif*, 311 (January), 18.

Thompson, K. (1998) *Breaking the Glass Armour* (Princeton: Princeton University Press).

Toffetti, S. (1998) 'Moretti entre fioretti et comédie italienne, *Cahiers du cinéma*, 524 (May), 66–8.

Toubiana, S. (1989a) 'Entretien avec Nanni Moretti', *Cahiers du cinéma*, 425 (November), 22–32.

_____ (1989b) 'Le regard moral. *Palombella rossa*', *Cahiers du cinéma*, 425 (November), 20–1.

Tudor, A. (1989) *Monsters and Mad Scientists* (Blackwell: Oxford).

Valens, G. (1999) '*La cosa* and *La premiere de Close-Up*', *Positif*, 464 (October), 174–5.

Vecchi, P. (1981) '*Sogni d'oro* di Nanni Moretti', *Cineforum*, 208 (October), 64–7.

Vergerio, F. (1990) 'Venezia 81. Film in concorso', *Rivista del cinematografo*, September/October 1981, reprinted in P. Ugo & A. Floris (eds) *Facciamoci del male. Il cinema di Nanni Moretti* (Cagliari: CUEC).

Villa, F. (1999) 'Oggi farò delle belle riprese, sì, anche se mi vergogno un po'. Percorso nel raccontar leggero', in *Nanni Moretti*, Garage. Cinema Autori Visioni (Torino: Paravia Scriptorium).

Wagstaff, C. (1999) '*Aprile*', *Sight and Sound*, April, 36.

Walker, J. A. (1993) *Art and Artists on Screen* (Manchester: Manchester University Press).

Wayne, M. (2001) *Political Film. The Dialectics of Third Cinema* (London & Sterling, VA: Pluto Press).

Willan, P. (2002) 'Italian court tells father to support stay-at-home son, 30', *Guardian*, 6 April, 2.

Wrobel, S. (2001) 'Biografia jako dzielo sztuki', *Sztuka i filozofia*, 19, 140–63.

Young, D. (2002a) 'Me, Myself, and Italy', *Film Comment*, January/February, 56–61.

_____ (2002b) 'First Look. *The Son's Room*', *Film Comment*, May/June, 74–5.

Zavattini, Cesare (1979) *Neorealismo ecc* (Milan: Bompiani).

INDEX